BRYANT: A CREEK INDIAN NATION TOWNSITE

BY

MICKEY J. "MIKE" MARTIN

THE FOWBLE PRESS

PUBLICATION DATA

PUBLISHER: Published in the United States of America by The Fowble Press, 3217 S. Thomas Street, Visalia, California 93292

RIGHTS:

LCCN: 2012942764

ISBN: 9780963827913 Hardcopy
9781478198956 Paperback

EDITION: Second Edition

*****

CONTENTS

ACKNOWLEDGMENTS

Research for this book began in 1990, the first edition was published in 1998, and the current edition was completed in 2012. Because the book is a collective memoir rather than a scholarly effort, it is a pleasure to recognize others whose memories helped make it possible. Information was obtained through direct discussion, letters or other forms of correspondence, and articles provided by former long-term residents of Bryant or their heirs, including but not limited to Sibyl Alice (Jones) Chancey, Martha B. (Davis) Schnabel, Homer Chancey, Connie Trafton, Ted Chancey, Guandina (Pippin) Pulliam, Mary Lou (Curtis) Sills, Pat (Chancey) Hernandez, Billie (Furr) Heckmaster, Darlene (Fish) Hames, Deloris (Popejoy) Adkins, Frank Crawford, Helen (French) Furr, Helen James, Jacklyn (Chancey) Houghton, Jackie (Pippin) (Goodson) Prince, Jim Meuhlhausen, Leona (Trover) George, Mary (Cathcart) Campbell, Virgie (Sanders) Poe, and many others; archived local newspaper articles; and memoirs created by Bryant School students that were collected, compiled, and distributed by Dorothy (West) Kizer at Bryant All School Reunions. Some of those who helped with the project have already passed away, but through their contributions they have played an important role in making sure that the Town of Bryant and Bryant School will be remembered!

Mike Martin

BRYANT: A CREEK INDIAN NATION TOWNSITE

by

MICKEY J. "MIKE" MARTIN

THE FOWBLE PRESS

CHAPTER 1

OPENING COMMENT

A dot still appears on some maps of Oklahoma to identify the location of Bryant, a now defunct small town that used to be one of the incorporated municipalities of Okmulgee County. Today, people live in and around the old town simply because they value the peace and serenity of quiet country living more highly than ready access to all the conveniences of living in a larger town. One point that can be taken for granted about these folks is that they sure didn't land at Bryant because they harbored any expectation of getting rich as a result of having moved there.

Surprisingly, though, expectations of doing precisely that—becoming financially well off—was exactly what drew people to Bryant in the old days, back when it was one of the many new town sites popping up on land that only a short time before had been the exclusive domain of the Creek Nation, way out in the Oklahoma Indian Territory. Those who took part in the town site development period of frontier Oklahoma were drawn to the Territory by the hope of economic betterment through land speculation, land development, land ownership, or some form of entrepreneurship, and most of them made no secret of their aspirations. Dreams of many different kinds drew people to old Bryant, but the one element all the dreamers had in common was a desire to pursue their own economic self-interests. Without a doubt, this was their common guiding light.

People who are curious about Oklahoma's town site development period want to know more about the identity and real life experiences of those who bought and sold property, cultivated farms, built up ranches, started businesses, or practiced trades or crafts in and around places like Bryant, towns that sprang into being during this unique period in our national history. Goings-on in the Territory captured attention back when they were taking place, and they continue to do so today. Today, though, people want to know about more than the exploits of Wild West outlaws or the near-mythical figures of those times, as interesting as that side of the history of Oklahoma may be; they want to know how the actual settlers of towns like Bryant fared during their day-to-day lives, and how things turned out for them in the end. In other words, they want to know what happened to the residents of Bryant after the initial euphoria of settling in the exotic-sounding Oklahoma Indian Territory finally wore off. Providing answers to questions of this kind is, in a nutshell, what this book is all about.

Through the use of short historical overviews, selected personal commentaries, reviews of old documents, presentation of unique non-stock period photographs, and brief recitations of personal experiences, this book amounts to an attempt to illustrate what life was like for many of those whose daily experiences make up the history of Bryant. Those who settled in and around this particular little farm town were no more than folks who were doing the best they could to build solid futures for their families, which means that they surely didn't think of themselves as being in any way remarkable when they lived there. Today, though, we look upon their experiences as being personally fascinating, historically significant, and in many ways surprisingly instructive in terms of many things we need to be careful about as we live the far more insulated and comfortable lives that are common in our times.

To understand the forces that attracted people to Bryant as a place to settle, it is necessary to learn a bit about the history of the area in which the town is located. The more that is known about the area in which any town is located, the more alive the history of the place becomes. Without some understanding of the historical facts that gave rise to a town's existence, it is far too easy to minimize the role it and other places just like it played in the way our nation developed. As we strive to meet the challenges of our own times, there is value in recalling with all the respect that the period rightfully deserves the unique experiences that played out at places like Bryant. There were many small farm towns just like it in the Oklahoma Indian Territory of the old days, and records like this one are needed to tell their individual stories.

Many small farm towns were devastated as our nation went through a relatively rapid transition from an agricultural to an industrial economy, and studying their economic experiences can provide insights that may help us deal with the even more difficult transition of our own times—our move from an industrial to an information-based economy. Let's hope so, since it has become abundantly clear that we're going to need all the help we can get!

A few Oklahoma Indian Territory town sites succeeded beyond all expectations, but most of them went through periods of great struggle just to survive. Many of them, in fact, did not survive. Bryant, for example, started off with a bang, but then gradually faded away as an economically viable municipality. In the process, though, it became the base of experience upon which many of its residents went on to build happy and successful lives. The way life played out at Bryant is typical of how it played out for the residents of lots of other town sites just like it, and that, of course, is what makes study of the little town interesting and rewarding and of historical importance!

CHAPTER 2

BEFORE THE EARLY 1800'S

Before the early 1800s, the only inhabitants of the geographical area within which the Town of Bryant eventually came to be located were members of roaming bands of native (or *wild*) Indians, people who sustained themselves primarily through hunting rather than through farming or any other approach to making a living that kept them settled at any one location. Primarily, they lived off the game animals that were at the time plentiful in their un-bordered and thinly populated region of the country. Even those who kept semi-permanent villages and raised a few garden crops still wandered from place to place in search of the animals that were their principal source of food, clothing, and shelter.

ORIGINAL INDIAN TRIBAL AREAS

Note that this map covers a long span of time, about 1250 A.D. to 1900 A.D. Not all of the tribes shown lived in the same time period—some of them developed at a later date, and territories shifted over the years.

SOURCE: Land of Promise: A History of the United States from 1865, Volume 2, by Carol Berkin and Leonard Wood, Copyright© 1986. Pearson Education for Its Affiliates. Used by permission. All Rights Reserved.

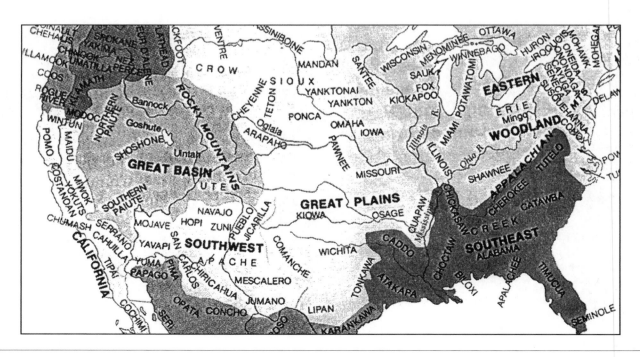

Members of the tribes of the area thought of themselves as *land users* rather than *land owners*, even to the extent of believing that no individual or group had a right to *own* the land, creeks, rivers, or the privilege of hunting wild game. Instead, they believed that every man ought to be free to wander wherever his strengths and interests might take him. Sadly for native tribal people, however, whites who showed up in later years in search of homesteads interpreted these very attitudes and values to mean that Native American areas were *unclaimed* and, therefore, available to anyone who willing to work hard to settle them. Clashes between Native Americans and whites were inevitable as westward expansion took place in our country, and native Indians pretty much always ended up on the short end of the stick. Over the years, one by one the native tribes that lived in the area around where the Town of Bryant would late be located were forced to live settled lives on reservation land that was set aside for them in what the federal government referred to as *The Indian Territory*.

NATIVE (OR "WILD") VERSUS "CIVILIZED" INDIANS

Before eastern (or "civilized") Indian tribes were "resettled" in the area around where Bryant came to be located, it was the domain of members of native (or "wild") Indian tribes such as these Arapahos. There were great differences between various tribal peoples, and it was not uncommon for members of native tribes to resent the relocation of eastern tribes to territory they considered their own.

SOURCE: National Anthropological Archives, Smithsonian Institution Item #01623301. Used with permission.

CHAPTER 3

"RELOCATION" OF THE SOUTHEASTERN CREEK INDIANS

The first population group to permanently settle—or, more accurately, to *be* permanently settled—in the Indian Territory area within which the Town of Bryant came to be located were the Creek Indians of the southeastern states of Alabama, Georgia, and the Carolinas. Their *relocation* came about when the federal government forcibly moved—or *resettled*, as it was described back then—them from their tribal homelands in these states during the early 1800s.

Because the Creek Indians played such an important role in the development Town of Bryant, it is necessary to know something about these Indians to fully understand how the town came into being. Their tribal story must begin with a brief explanation of how and why it came to be believed that their tribe needed to be *resettled* in the first place. Their history is well known to historians, and many excellent accounts of it are in existence. One of the best of these accounts has been provided by Michael D. Green in an excellent study called *The Politics of Indian Removal,* an overview of which is a principal reference for the following pages of this chapter. For purposes of this narrative, just a brief overview of how the Creek Indian tribe came to be resettled in the Oklahoma Indian Territory will suffice.

EARLY CREEK CONTACT WITH EUROPEANS

A long relationship had existed between the Creek people and white explorers, traders, and settlers of the southeastern part of our country during the early pioneer period before the tribe was *removed* to the Indian Territory, but it was never a particularly positive or happy one. Long before the Creeks were forced off the land they had occupied for as long as could be remembered in Alabama, Georgia, and parts of the Carolinas, they had in several significant ways been negatively impacted by their contact with Europeans. Early on, for example, as was the case for so many other Indian tribes, their lack of immunity to diseases such as small pox, measles, influenza, and others caused them misery and death at a level we can hardly imagine today.

The very earliest explorers to Creek tribal areas in the southeastern United States recorded, for example, that there had been *pests* (or diseases) in the land and that everywhere they had seen large, vacant towns, grown up in grass, places where whole groups of Indians had died off. When Fernando De Soto's men arrived years later, they brought with them even more diseases for which the Indians had no immunities. Twenty years after some of their earliest contacts with whites, the western part of the original Creek territory, which as far back as the 1540s had been densely settled, was nearly depopulated. All their contacts with Spanish and other European explorers, traders, settlers, and missionaries during the sixteenth and seventeenth centuries brought diseases that continued to exact a toll on the Indians throughout the years that followed.

It has been estimated that regional epidemics that occurred in 1696-98, 1738-39, 1759-60, 1779-80, and as late as 1831 killed off a huge number of the Native Indian population of the southeastern United States. At no time before their forced removal from their native homelands were the Creeks ever free of epidemic diseases of one kind or another, all caused by their contact with whites. Some researchers have estimated that as many as nineteen out of twenty Native Indians died of epidemic diseases within the first two centuries because of their contact with whites. As hard as it may be for us to believe this today, that's what the experts say.

After the explorations of De Soto and others paved the way, more whites of various nationalities moved into areas that had once been occupied only by the southeastern Creeks. By 1700, Creek Indians were in direct and frequent contact with Spanish settlers in Florida, French settlers in Louisiana, and British settlers in the Carolinas, and, at first, these relationships between Indians and whites seemed to be mutually beneficial.

During these early years, economics dominated all relationships between natives and whites. Both sides actively pursued trade and both benefited, at least initially, from the barter of deer hides and captive Indians (who were sold into slavery) for guns, powder, and the various manufactured goods whites used as trade items. For the Creeks, however, the full ramifications of their interaction with whites did not become apparent until after a long association with them.

One of the most basic changes that affected Creek society had to do with their acquisition of manufactured goods. The iron and steel tools and weapons that were traded by the whites for deerskins, furs, and captives dramatically changed the way Creek men spent their time. For example, handmade deerskin clothing was replaced by cloth clothing and guns replaced bows and arrows for use in hunting and fighting.

What ultimately came to pass among the Creeks was that reliance on the new trade goods provided by the whites evolved into a dependence that became so debilitating that they lost their ability to defend their land when white demand for more territory began to grow. The time saved by the great reduction in labor hours devoted to hand making domestic goods wound up being absorbed by a major increase in the production of deer hides, the Creek nation's principal medium of exchange in trade, and by increased warfare on neighboring tribes to acquire captives for the slave market. Hides and slaves were the major items the Creeks traded to whites to get the manufactured goods they wanted.

Originally, Creek men hunted only for their own food and they tended to stay relatively close to their home area, but when their appetite for manufactured goods started to grow, Creek hunters found that they had to spend more time hunting and traveling further from home to find deer. This had the effect of increasing their hostile contacts with tribes that lived near them and causing them to compete all the more aggressively with them for a finite number of deer.

The profit motive that had been introduced by white traders also changed the very nature of Creek warfare. At one time, they had fought against other Indians only sporadically and in retaliation for offenses against their nation. The Creeks now began to make large-scale invasions into the territories of other tribes for the sole purpose of capturing prisoners to be sold to slave traders. The profits they earned from slaving were enough to make the business worthwhile, but it has been estimated that as many as three Indians died for every one that was successfully captured for the market. Creek men became, in effect, commercial hunters and slave raiders, and became less and less involved with agriculture and other domestic affairs than ever before.

Most Creek towns during these early years of contact with whites had one or more white traders in residence. These traders built stores and houses, kept herds of cattle, horses, and hogs, married Creek women, and raised bilingual and bicultural mixed-blood children. For most of the year the traders sold goods on credit, collecting payment in tanned hides in the spring. Creek trade centered on replacing items that they formerly hand-made for themselves with manufactured goods made by whites.

RELATIONS DISINTEGRATE BETWEEN CREEKS AND WHITES

As time passed, relations between the Creeks and whites became strained over Creek leaders' concerns with unregulated and unethical traders and unrestrained squatters moving into their territory. The state and federal governments of the time made token attempts to deal with these problems, but pressure from white settlers, traders, and politicians was such that they found it an almost hopeless task. White leaders in Alabama and Georgia were far more interested in doing whatever they could to take land away from the native Indians than in protecting their rightful claims to it.

Many whites of those times were contemptuous of native Indians and their property rights, and some were downright cruel, dishonest, and greedy in their relations with them. Most of the traders did not respect the Indians nor were they in turn respected, but the parties put up with each other because both sides mutually benefited from their trade relationships. The Indians came to look upon any whites in their territory that were of no direct benefit to them as enemies whose encroachments and abuses demanded resistance.

However legitimate they may have been, the complaints of the Creeks against the early white settlers and traders in their homelands were met more with platitudes than with any real solutions. Land was the real issue, and the only interaction whites were really interested in was for the Creeks to sell off their land for legal occupation by settlers and developers. White leaders creatively plotted and schemed to find any and every way they could to get the Indians off their land. Little by little, Creek headmen began to sell or barter away pieces of land in exchange for peace and quiet and basic personal safety. Whatever they did, however, was never enough; the white settlers wanted everything for themselves.

THE FIRST RESPONSE OF THE CREEKS

Ultimately realizing that white encroachment would be a perpetual and ever increasing threat to their independence and territorial claims, Creek leaders tried to rally their people into a stronger tribal association that would give them some protection against white expansionism. The Creek Indians of Georgia and Alabama eventually did successfully organize their independent and autonomous tribes into a Confederacy that developed some of the attributes of a true national government. Internal political dissention, however, kept them from ever becoming as effective as they could have been.

Upon realizing that their people were threatened with the prospect of literally being overrun by white settlers, Creek leaders did all they could to protect their people and preserve their values and way of life. They fought for concessions, stalled for time during negotiations with whites, and tried as hard as they could to bridge the gaps between all the many factions and special interest groups that existed among their own people. Factionalism, disunity, what has been called *particularism*, and obsessive local loyalties, however, all combined to prevent the Nation from combating the encroachment of whites.

Eventually, most Creeks leaders came to believe that the only way to deal with whites was to learn from their culture, especially their political organization, and to make adaptations that were necessary to coexist with the more powerful white culture and institutions. By building a strong and politically single-minded Creek Nation, they believed they could protect their land and stop the influx of white settlers. They won some time and many concessions for their people, but ultimately a diminished sense of clan community and the introduction of *civilized* concepts had the effect of breaking down Creek tribal unity and creating what was described as a *spirit of individuality* (or *non-tribalness*) that added to the internal weakness of their Nation.

The Creeks, in other words, were at least partly forced into a position of having to adopt white ways. In the face of the possibility of being overwhelmed by whites, many hunters followed the lead of the mixed-blood members of their tribe and the advice of government agents and adopted some form of plow agriculture. Those unwilling or unable to make this transition attempted to live on annuity income derived from the land sales. Many, however, steadfastly opposed efforts to turn themselves into plow farmers, just as they opposed anything that might put them in a position of having white civilization forced on them.

During these times, even many whites who felt genuine concern for their plight felt a paternalistic moral and economic imperative to promote *civilization* among the Indians. As far as the state and federal governments of the day were concerned, however, civilization meant plow agriculture practiced on small, individually owned plots of land. The prevailing belief of the time was that the earth had been given to mankind to support the greatest number of which it is capable, and no tribe or people had a right to keep from the wants of others more than was necessary for their own support and comfort. In other words, what most whites really believed was that the Creeks had no right to claim continued ownership of any land that they did not settle and farm.

Believing that training native people in plow agriculture and settling them on personal plots of land would release thousands of acres of *surplus* land for white settlement, Congress enacted the Civilization Fund Act of 1819. The law provided funds for the instruction of Native people in ways of agriculture that were suited to their situation, and for teaching their children to read, write, and do arithmetic. The real purpose of the civilization law, however, was to enable the government to, in effect, educate Native people off their land. In pursuit of this goal, the government provided funding to missionary societies to help pay for the construction and maintenance of new Indian schools and to pay the salaries of teachers. In return for this it was understood that the missionaries would support government measures designed to deal with the tribes. Through this unspoken system, the mission societies effectively became semi-official agencies of the federal government.

Contrary to what state and federal government officials really expected to happen, the *civilization* policy worked out very well in terms of the interests of the Indians but not very well at all in terms of their own unstated desires. As the Indians became educated according to white laws and standards and became more interested in participating in the economic system of the whites, they became more skillful at resisting the manipulations of government efforts that were focused on depriving them of their land. The so-called *Civilized Indians* (five tribes were so thought of), in effect, came to understand the true value of their land and therefore resisted efforts to part them from it.

The civilization program ended up becoming a kind of double-edged sword for white people. They thought that educating the Indians would eventually help get them off their land, but instead it acted to increase their resistance. Frustrated by what was happening, some white leaders began to advocate a more direct means of opening Indian land for white settlement—denying the sovereignty of the Indian nations, scrapping the treaty system, imposing full congressional control, and condemning Indian lands through the exercise of eminent domain.

Justifying their views by claiming a need to protect whites from Indian attacks, white leaders effectively argued that the military security of the southeast region needed a permanent population of whites who would be able to defend it. Military leaders of the day complained that if the Indians were the subjects of the United States inhabiting its territory and acknowledging its sovereignty, then wasn't it absurd for the sovereign to negotiate by treaty with the subject? Native people were entitled to protection and fostering care by the government, but no more so than other American citizens. These *citizens* were, therefore, subject to the laws of Congress, just like everybody else.

The Creeks were effectively being forced into accepting land allotments, then manipulated into either giving up or selling for a pittance their land rights as allottees and, further, being *removed* to the far west to land where they could finally be free from harassment by whites. Many Creeks leaders, however, did not support the sale of their land or the idea of moving to an unknown area west of the Mississippi. The Creek Council refused to renegotiate their land rights as provided by existing treaties, and instead demanded their enforcement as promised.

The Creeks pleaded with the government to expel *illegal* squatters from their treaty land, but instead the squatters only became more insistent. For federal and state government officials of the time, the route of escape from the complaints and controversy stemming from friction between settlers and the Indians lay in the *removal* of the Creeks to the West. Many considered the protective clauses of the various Indian treaties with contempt, even considering the various land allotment plans under consideration at the time to be little more than elaborate bribes to the headmen and families of the Creek Nation to get the Indians off their land. They fully expected that the Creeks, once they had their allotments, would immediately sell them to whites, pocket the money, and leave the area.

No one expected or wanted the Creeks to stay in their home areas as independent land-owning citizens of the states. What the whites really wanted was for the Creeks to voluntarily *remove* from their homeland to be resettled beyond the Mississippi River in areas that were wild, unsettled, and, at that time, unwanted and unclaimed by anyone other than the government. Most of the Creeks probably had no interest in becoming permanent citizens of the white southern states, but neither did they want to give up their land and leave for an uncertain future in what to them was a wild and unknown place.

Since it would not accomplish their overall objective if only small groups of Creeks agreed to give up their land while the majority wanted to stay put, white officials became more and more frustrated with *the Indian situation*. Not willing to patiently wait for a better solution, whites began doing all they could to dislodge the Indians from land they had lived on for longer than anyone knew. Eventually, they hoped to provoke certain groups of Indians into hostility in order to justify military intervention to break what was seen as a stalemate in terms of dealing with the *Indian problem*.

Little by little with the passage of time, bits and pieces of Indian land were wrested away until it came to a point where the whole of their remaining land was individual property and they had little or no bargaining power left as an independent nation. The Indian people were still there, but their national land rights were gone. Their communal land had become *individual property* in the eyes of whites, a concept that only a few of the Creeks really understood and truly supported. The majority of the Creeks were eventually forced into homelessness and near starvation.

THE DESPERATE SECOND RESPONSE OF THE CREEKS

Driven by want and frustration and the knowledge that they were being robbed by whites of land they had lived on for generations, many members of the Creek tribe decided to fight back. Those who were politically aware knew they had very little chance of winning any armed conflict with whites, but they felt their only choice was to fight for what they had left or loose everything. When they did, soldiers and militiamen were called up *for the suppression of hostilities in the Creek country* and to demand the *unconditional submission of the Indians* so that they could be disarmed and *resettled* as fast as this could be accomplished. Whether hostile or friendly, all Creeks were to be transported west—by military force if necessary.

As the inevitable played out, the United States Army brought about in a few months what politicians and treaty talks had failed for many years to achieve. Their defeat in the Creek War of 1813-14 effectively ended the military power of the southeastern Creek Indians. From 1814 to 1836, the year of their final removal to the west, the Creek Indians remained under continual pressure from the Georgia, Alabama, and United States governments to give up their native homelands. Their defeat in the war and the growing power of white settlers made further armed resistance impossible, and the Creeks (like all the other eastern Indian tribes) were forced to leave their home area for resettlement in the newly-created Oklahoma Indian Territory.

"*REMOVAL*" TO THE INDIAN TERRITORY

The United States Government forcibly *removed* the Creek tribe, along with four other so-called *civilized* tribes (the Choctaw, Chickasaw, Cherokee and Seminole), over what the Cherokees came to call the *Trail of Tears* to *Indian Territory*, or what is now Eastern Oklahoma. Forced migrations occurred in the 1820s as well as the 1830s. A series of different groups, a total of around 19,609 Creeks, were eventually resettled in the new land, of which the federal War Department classified around 2,500 as *hostile*. Hundreds of those who were resettled died of hunger, disease, and exposure before their trip west was completed. Those who did reach Indian Territory were settled in what is now the State of Oklahoma, ragged and miserable and demoralized. In the end, only a handful of Creeks were left in their native area.

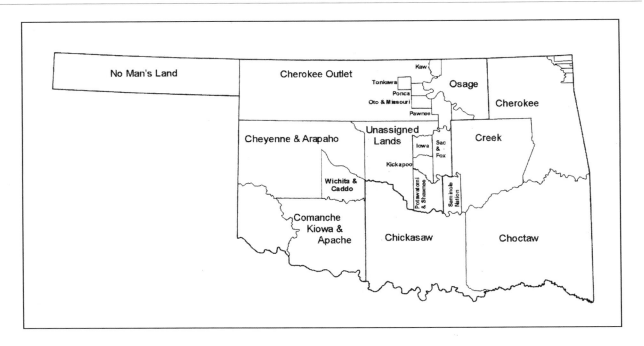

THE OKLAHOMA INDIAN TERRITORY
FROM 1866 TO 1889

THE CREEK INDIAN NATION IN 1898

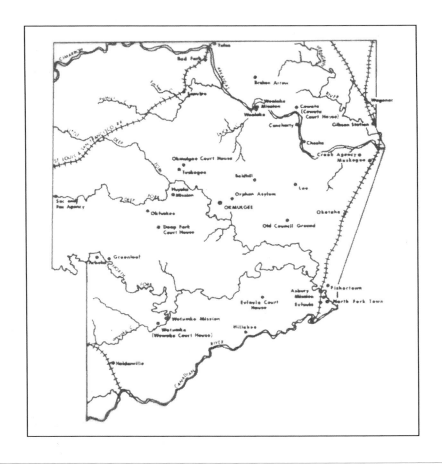

CHAPTER 4

THE CREEK NATION, I. T.

Once they were resettled on their new land out in the Indian Territory, the Creeks realized they had no choice but to do whatever had to be done to make the best of a bad situation. They didn't like the great change that had been forced upon them, but they thought that in their newly assigned land they would at least be left alone to live their lives free of white interference. Because they were declared free to carry on as citizens of their own sovereign if not actually totally independent nation within the borders of the United States, they began to make their own laws, handle their own law enforcement, conduct government operations, and generally handle their affairs as any small but independent country would. A center of tribal activity was established where the Town of Okmulgee (named after Ocmulgee, Georgia) is located today, and, in later years, they declared the town their national capitol.

The area within the Indian Territory set aside for the new Creek Indian Nation encompassed parts of Rogers, Mayes, Creek, Tulsa, Wagoner, Cherokee, Okmulgee, Muskogee, Okfuskee, McIntosh, Seminole, and Hughes counties after Oklahoma became the 46th State of the Union on November 16 of 1907, but back when the tribe was relocated there it was widely thought as a wild and desolate place. Even so, the land areas that were set aside for the various tribes were to be protected in perpetuity from interference by outsiders, and treaties signed by the federal government and the tribes promised the Indians, including the Creeks, rights that were supposed to be parallel with those of independent nations. Territorial borders, the Indians were promised, would be respected as well as protected.

It all sounded good on paper, but, sadly for the Creeks as well as other tribes, despite the many promises of the federal government, white and black settlers continually (and illegally) pushed their way onto tribal land in the Indian Territory anyway, ignoring treaties and Indian rights. As their new tribal area became better established, trading posts and then small settlements that included white and black as well as Creek Indian inhabitants began to form at various locations within their nation. What confused the situation even more is that the resettled tribes, including the Creeks, leased some of their land to settlers for use as ranches and farms.

All through the 1850s and beyond, powerful interest groups such as cattlemen and railroad companies pressured the federal government to open any and all specifically unassigned areas in the Territory for access and development. Many Indians leaders realized what continued intrusion on the part of whites would mean to their race and to their claims against the land, but they weren't well enough organized to muster enough political power to change the course of events they saw taking place right before their eyes.

Creek Indian household near Bryant

Creek woman on a wagon

Creek Indian hunters in the 1910s

Young Creek women in the early 1900s

Creek Indian rodeo star performer Senora Burgess in 1911

Creek Indian Frankie Martin – Exact Year Unknown

CHAPTER 5

THE LAND ALLOTMENT PROGRAM

When the Civil War ended in 1866, the federal government insisted that the various resettled Indian tribes renegotiate their land treaties as compensation for the fact that the majority of them had sided with the South against the North during the war. Renegotiating their treaties, the government had concluded, would be an expedient way to penalize the Indians and, at the same time, create a place to settle many of the black slaves freed after the War as well as open more land for white settlement.

Even though the overall amount of land set aside for reservations was being reduced through the negotiation of new treaties, even more Indian tribes were resettled in the Indian Territory over the years that followed. As this was going on, the so-called *Cherokee Strip* on the northern border as well as a much valued area in the center of Oklahoma, which were still not assigned any specific use, came to be referred to as *unassigned lands* that were much coveted by prospective settlers. They began to call these areas—and, in fact, all of Indian Territory—*the promised land*, due to the opportunity it offered for livestock grazing and the possibility converting it into free land that could be made available for homesteading.

The federal government's mechanism for dealing with the situation was the Dawes Act of 1887, which was passed by Congress to deal with the tribes that had been confined to reservations. The Act was very pointedly designed to bring an end to tribal life and to convert Indians to white peoples' ways. The tribes themselves were dissolved, and tribal ownership of lands was ended. Individual land ownership, a concept that was unfamiliar to the Indians and still not supported by many of them, was put in place by allotting to each married Indian male 160 acres and each adult single man or woman 80 acres of land, land to be used for farming or grazing. Freed blacks who had moved to the Indian Territory were conveniently dealt with by designating them *adoptees* of the various tribes as a means of justifying giving them the same land allotment rights the Indians received.

Once land was placed in the hands of individual allottees, they had a right (with some restrictions) to resell or transfer their property or property rights as they so desired. At the same time, other provisions of the Act made it possible for non-Indians to settle on any land that was not allotted to individual Indians. Because many Indians did not know how to profitably deal with all the changes that were put into effect, the end result of the allotment system was that many

Indian hunters-forced-to-turn-farmers were cheated out of much of their land by grasping whites. A good number of Indians, in fact, ended up both landless and penniless. That a great loss of Indian land resulted from the changes that were made is confirmed by actual figures. In 1873, at the beginning of the reservation policy, the Indian reservations contained about 150 million acres; in 1887, when the Dawes Act was passed, the amount had dropped to 138 million acres; and, eventually, by 1934, when the Dawes Act was repealed, the Indians ended up with only 52 million acres of land.

The present-day State of Oklahoma was divided into two governmental divisions and four sections in May of 1890. Indian Territory encompassed all of the eastern one-third of the State and the Cherokee Outlet; Oklahoma Territory included the panhandle, or *No Man's Land*, and an area which stretched northeast from the southwestern section to the Kansas border, called *Unassigned Lands*, dividing the two sections of Indian land. Further responding to even more demand for land for white settlement, additional areas were opened to homesteading in 1891, 1893, 1895, 1901, and 1906. Though some did make illegal *Sooner* homestead claims, the majority of white settlers in the territory of Oklahoma obtained their lands through entirely legal means.

Despite the objections of the various Indian tribes, by 1900 *Oklahoma Territory* had been expanded to encompass the entire western half of the present-day State and even more. At the same time, *Indian Territory* was gradually reduced to the eastern section. It was abundantly clear to anyone with good political awareness that the days of the Indian Territory were numbered and that residents of the Oklahoma Territory were likely to push for statehood at some point in the near future. In all but name only, the transition from *Indian Territory* to *Oklahoma Territory* had been completed.

DAWES COMMISSION MEMBERS AT A MEETING

GROUP PICTURE AT A FAMILY GATHERING IN 1903

ALLOTMENT LAND WITHIN SECTION 32, TOWNSHIP 11 NORTH, RANGE 12 EAST, CREEK NATION, I. T.

NOTE: This map shows the location of allotment land owned by Joshua Asbury, a Creek Indian who played an important role in the development of Bryant.

SOURCE: Hastain's Township Plats of the Creek

CHAPTER 6

ARRIVAL OF THE RAILROADS

It was the extension of rail service into the once isolated Indian Territory that made the Town of Bryant an economically viable proposition. Without access to rail transportation, many of the town sites that sprang up in Oklahoma would never have been developed—or, at the very least, not developed until many years later than they were. It was for the express purpose of linking these remote areas to the rest of the country that the federal government actively began to support the construction efforts of first large railroad companies and then regional lines back in the late 1800s.

Before rail transportation became available, our whole country was made up of thousands of little economic islands—communities that were isolated from each other not just by differing interests but by physical distance. Traveling was difficult, time consuming, and expensive. Most people lived in small towns, places where they personally knew almost everyone who lived around them. In fact, most knew everyone in their town by name—not to mention the names of everyone else's spouse, sons, daughters, parents, and grandparents. The world most people occupied back then was not a large place.

In the 1860s and 1870s prior to the coming of the rail lines that were to so dramatically change our nation, the United States was still a country made up of small farmers who lived off their own land, of independent craftsmen who made one of a kind products in their own workshops, and of small entrepreneurs who ran their own businesses. The major eastern cities of our country were connected by railroad lines, but it was not possible to go to the west coast by train. Railway maps of the period would have shown a detailed system of railroad tracks in the eastern part of the United States, but from Chicago to the west the map would have been almost totally blank. To get to California or other towns on the Pacific Coast or to send mail there took months of hard travel over mountains and across deserts or a sea trip around Cape Horn.

This situation was changed forever, when, during the Civil War, the federal government saw a need for a faster way to travel to the western part of the United States for the purpose of moving troops and military supplies. This was a major impetus for Congress moving to unify the nation by building a railroad system that would cross the entire country. As a mechanism for making this happen as quickly as possible, in 1862 it chartered the construction of two transcontinental railroad lines—the Union Pacific Railroad, which was to build a track from Omaha,

Nebraska, to Utah, and the Central Pacific Railroad, was to build a track from Sacramento, California, to Utah.

To accelerate the work of the two rail companies, the federal government subsidized their projects by providing them with loans and land grants. Each company was given, for example, loans of $16,000 for every mile of track laid on flat land and $48,000 for each mile over mountainous terrain. Public land on both sides of the rail route was divided up in a checkerboard pattern, with the government reserving alternate tracts, each 20 miles square, for the railroad companies' use. In return for the aid they received, the railroads agreed to transport federal troops and federal mail at reduced rates. The meeting of the two lines at Promontory Point in Utah on May 10, 1869, marked the completion of our country's first transcontinental railway. It now became possible to make a trip across America in the formerly impossible time of one week, a fact that was considered amazing at the time.

The success of the transcontinental railroad projects created an immediate rush of railway construction by other railroad companies. By the 1890s there were four more lines extending from the Midwest to the Pacific Coast: the Southern Pacific, the Northern Pacific, the Great Northern, and the Atchison, Topeka & Santa Fe. These major routes, which were called *trunk lines*, however, were not the only railroads built during this period of time. Less than 35,000 total miles of track were laid in 1865, but the amount increased to 52,000 in 1870, 74,000 in 1875, and 167,000 miles of track in 1890. These construction figures included hundreds of feeder lines that connected local towns and cities to the major trunk lines.

The federal government's railroad land grant program helped in the building of almost all of these rail lines. The railroads used their land grants not only to build tracks, but also to resell land to settlers and businesses as yet another means of making money off the westward expansion of our country. It was in these ways that the railroads helped to populate the West. They made their land especially attractive to customers, often by offering low fares to people interested in buying western property. By 1890, a joint effort of the Chicago, Rock Island, and Pacific, and the Atchison, Topeka, and Santa Fe railroad companies had completed a railroad line from Guthrie to Kingfisher and beyond to Seward.

Access by rail was extended into the area in which the Town of Bryant eventually came to be located in 1898, when the Frisco Railroad began surveying to lay spur lines to the Creek Mining Company coal mines that dotted the local landside. It was for the purpose of hauling coal from these mines that the Frisco Railroad wanted to lay track through this part of the Creek Nation.

Railroad owners of these times had to negotiate with individual Creek landowners for rights to lay track for the spur lines that were necessary to load cars and get them ready for transport. Some of the first track into the area where Bryant came to be located was put down on land owned by a man by the name Joshua Asbury, a Creek Indian (but perhaps not a full blood) who had received it through the federal government's land allotment program. His allotment land was located in the southwestern portion of Okmulgee County, about five miles southwest of Henryetta.

Before the turn of the century, Asbury's area was thickly populated by members of his tribe, Creek Indians who earned their living either as farmers or ranchers or miners. The Creek Mining Company had tapped surface layers and sunk shafts all around to extract the coal deposits that had been found in the hills and lying along creek beds in the area, and a good number of Creek men were employed as workers in these mines. Hoping to earn a good profit on his allotment acreage, Asbury became one of a number of Creeks who made agreements with a Frisco Railroad representative, a *road master* by the last name of Bryant, to allow railroad right-of-way across their land—in Asbury's case, a 160-acre spread. By the end of the year 1900, a railroad line ran right by the site where the Town of Bryant would soon come to be located.

After the workers who had camped on his property while the spur line was being built moved on to other locations, Asbury's only remaining neighbors once again became other members of his tribe. Dave Barnett and his brother Jackson, for example, were among those who lived nearby. Jackson became famous in later years when a pool of oil was discovered on his allotment land, one that was rich enough to make him the wealthiest Indian in the United States.

Among Asbury's other Creek neighbors were Billy West and his family, people who lived near the location of the new railroad switch. In his earlier years, Billy had been a member of the famed Light horsemen Indian Police. His brother Lumpsy, who was a medicine man, was also well known in their area. Two other Indians who lived near Asbury were Jim Fisher and Dave W. Fields. Fields, who was an Indian preacher, opened a store later on and ended up becoming well known by everyone in the area. It has been said by some that an example of the advice he gave to people was to sleep in a cemetery if they had too much to drink, just so no one would come in to bother you.

In relatively short order, every Creek Indian resident was affected by the extension of rail transportation into the area, some much more quickly and significantly than others. In time, of course, every resident of Oklahoma was affected by the growth and expansion of the regional rail system, which made development possible where it hadn't been possible before. There's no doubt that it was the extension of rail service that brought about the great boom in the number of homestead claims that were filed in the State during the years that followed.

A railroad construction crew near Sapulpa in the 1900s

Raymond Duke, in front of the Frisco Railroad passenger station at Bryant in 1929. No better photograph of the Depot at Bryant could be located.

CHAPTER 7

BRYANT, CREEK NATION, I.T.

Immediately after the federal land allotment program was implemented and access into the area became possible by rail, Indian Territory land that only a short time before was too remote for profitable exploitation suddenly became hot property. Investors and speculators as well as legitimate developers and serious long-term settlers had been waiting in the wings, so to speak, all anxious to take advantage of the opportunities that had become available out in the Indian Territory—an ambition, by the way, that was shared by a good number of Indian allotment land holders.

Creek Indian Joshua Asbury, for example, found yet another way to draw further income out of the allotment land that had been awarded to him: He made legal arrangements to lease some of it out for the purpose of white settlement. The land he leased out was legally identified as being within the northwest quarter of Section 32, Range 11 and 12 East, encompassing all sides of the railroad right-of-way. At around the same time, Asbury gave away as much as 120 acres of his land as well, land upon which, with his blessing, civic development could begin in earnest.

Very shortly thereafter, a local school teacher by the name of Logan Harper laid out the streets of a new town. It was named Bryant, after the Frisco Railroad road master Asbury worked with to arrange his various land deals. Once the town site was surveyed and land was divided into equal blocks, even more settlers were drawn to the area. Then, to meet the needs of all the new white settlers who were moving into the town or the surrounding area, Harper began to push for the construction of a subscription school. It, too, when it was built, was located on part of the 120 acres donated by Asbury.

According to some old-time residents, the Stephans were the first white family to settle at Bryant, and they are credited with building the first home at the new town site. Not long thereafter, a settler known as *Mr. Bigney* opened a store and sawmill, both of which were located at a site just outside the Asbury property line. In 1904, Bigney sold out to Lloyd Tindall. Also in 1904, a man by the name of Les Martin opened a second store. Years later, Martin became the town's second postmaster.

By the time an official post office was established at Bryant on September 24, 1904, about forty families were living in or around the town site. (Note that an unofficial post office was opened in 1901.) The official first post office was located in the home of a man by the name of George Halick Burroughs, who became the town's first postmaster. Mail was addressed to *Bryant, Creek Nation, Indian Territory*, and all of it was delivered by train. Bryant's post office remained on the list of Okmulgee County post offices until it had to be closed down due to a declining local population. Since 1954, mail for Bryant has been routed through post offices in Henryetta or other nearby towns.

More jobs were added when the Victoria Mining Company opened in 1904. Located about three miles north of Bryant near the Frisco Railroad, it was mined by Italian, German, Bohemian, French, and Czech families. Mining was a major occupation in the area, at least for a number of years.

At this point, newly arriving settlers began to build homes, start farms and ranches, open new businesses, and raise new families. People were optimistic about their future prospects, since they thought they were well poised to become the beneficiaries of the prosperity that promoters had promised was possible in their exotic area, which, until only a short time before, had been set aside and reserved as *The Indian Territory*. Expectations of better times to come led public-spirited citizens to actively participate in various town-building activities. A town government was established, and interest grew in launching the subscription school Logan Harper had proposed. Town site organization and development was unsteady these early days, but progress was definitely being made.

Even more businesses were opened, and a cotton gin constructed by the Choctaw Cotton Oil and Milling Company provided a great economic boost for the town. The freight agent for the company, Cleo Ross, kept the Frisco Railroad Station busy during the cotton season. Agriculture and ranching were always important subsets of the local economy.

J. M. Herrin became the first mayor of Bryant, and W. A. "Bert" Wilkie became the first constable. Even as he grew to be noted as a strong lawman, Mr. Wilkie was also employed as a mine supervisor. The first city attorney was Mr. Connifax, who became Superintendent of Bryant Schools in later years. R. L. Alexander, who started a practice in 1915 and opened the town's first drug store, became Bryant's first doctor.

Because Bryant did not have a municipal water source, a man by the name of Leonard M. Duke became a very important person around town. Duke became important because he made extra money as a water hauler, selling water he delivered at a price of 50 cents per barrel. Bryant had no water source, sewer system, or sanitary services. In those days, people stored water in barrels or had their own cistern. Duke's full-time job was with the Victoria Mining Company, where he was a mule team driver for the mining company.

In 1921 when oil was discovered in the area, the population of Bryant temporarily ballooned to 2,600. There was lots of growth during the days of the *wildcatters*, and there was plenty of wealth in the area. It was during this time that Bryant finally became an incorporated town. Two new doctors also came to

Bryant in the early Twenties, twin brothers Clint and George M. Combest. Not long thereafter, a fourth doctor moved into the city, Dr. Holloway. Dr. Holloway shared an office with a man by the name of Rooney, who became Bryant's Justice of the Peace. In addition, a third drug store, called Fretwell's, was opened.

Three hotels were opened at around the same time, Mrs. McGraw's two-story fifteen-room McGraw Hotel, the single-story Fields Hotel with ten sleeping rooms, and the Crutchfield Hotel with an unknown number of rooms. In addition, two boarding houses were opened up—Alexander's Boarding House and Mrs. Jack J. Owens' Boarding House. During the Twenties, housing was in great demand.

In 1921 when he saw a need for a bank at Bryant, Henry Lee Chancey opened and became President of the First State Bank of Bryant. He hired a local couple by the name of Campbell to staff the bank. Mr. Campbell became his executive and Mrs. Campbell became his cashier. Chancey kept the bank in operation until 1926. He closed it down just after the oil boom began to fizzle out and just before the great stock market crash of 1929.

The city felt the full effects of the *oil boom* as oilfield workers combed the city streets in search of any sort of entertainment there was to be found. A dance hall built by a man by the name of Slim Crutchfield was among the businesses that were launched to meet the needs and wants of the *wildcatters* on paydays after the end of every long week of work. Crutchfield also owned the Crutchfield Hotel, Theater, and Restaurant. The dance hall became the scene of many arguments, fistfights, and gunfights. City Marshals "Bert" Wilkie during 1921 and "Baldy" Hughes during 1922 were kept busy in those days, sometimes to the extent of having to call in the county sheriff from the City of Okmulgee or state government-level officers to help quiet down trouble or to raid whiskey stills in the area.

Even though old-timers have noted that Bryant never had board or cement sidewalks alongside its streets, in its heyday it did have four lumber yards (Weeletka Lumber Company and Hardware, Southerland Lumber, Tulsa Rig and Reel Company, and another with a name that couldn't be found), a theater, a dance hall, several grocery stores (Jim Burns Grocery Store, W. A. Morgan's Meat Market, J. M. Herrin's Store, and Bryant Mercantile Store), Guggenheimer's Garage, Craig's Gas and Filling Station, four or five restaurants (among them the Blue Front Cafe, Drake's Café, the Good Eats Cafe, Mack's Cafe, and the Chile Parlor Cafe), a taxi service operated by Johnson Forrest, the hotel-boarding house operations mentioned before, Willingham's Feed and Seed Store, several oil field supply companies (Gypsy Oil Field Supply, Oklahoma Oil Field Supply Company, and Oil Well Supply of Bryant), and several other businesses. For seven or eight years during the boom years of the Twenties, it appeared that Bryant might become one of the leading towns of Okmulgee County. For most residents of the Town of Bryant, the Twenties ended up becoming the very best of times.

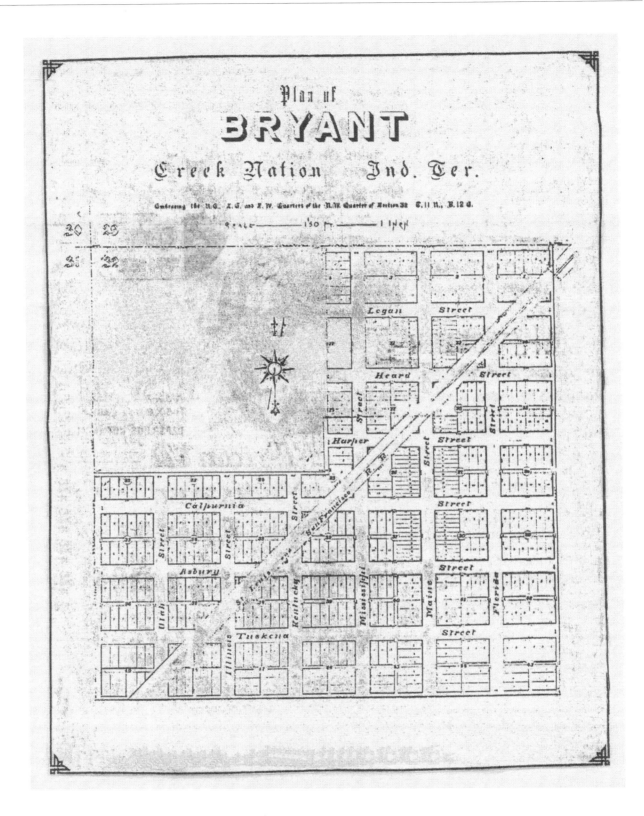

Original Indian Territory Plot Map
for the Town of Bryant

STREET NAMES OF BRYANT	
NORTH-SOUTH	EAST-WEST
Utah	Logan [1]
Illinois	Heard [2]
Kentucky	Harper [3]
Mississippi	Calpurnia [4]
Maine	Asbury [5]
Florida	Tuskonia [6]

1. Named after school teacher Logan Harper.

2. Named after an early settler.

3. Named after school teacher Logan Harper.

4. Named after Calpurnia, a daughter of plebeian (or common citizen) Calpurnius, who became one of Caesar's wives.

5. Named after Creek Indian Joshua Asbury.

6. A Creek Indian place or name.

##########

No. 1011.

(LOCATION PAPER.) *B*

Post Office Department,

OFFICE OF THE FOURTH ASSISTANT POSTMASTER GENERAL,
DIVISION OF APPOINTMENTS.

WASHINGTON, D. C., _____, 190 .

SIR: Before the Postmaster General decides upon the application for the establishment of a post office at _Bryant_, County of _Creek nation_, State of _Ind. Ter._, it will be necessary for you to carefully answer the subjoined questions, get a neighboring postmaster to certify to the correctness of the answers, and return the location paper to the Department, addressed to me.

If the site selected for the proposed office be not on any mail route, only a "Special Office" can be established, to be supplied with mail from some convenient point on the nearest mail route by a special carrier, for which service a sum equal two-thirds the salary of the postmaster will be paid by the Department. You should inform the contractor, or person performing service for him, of this application, and require him to execute the appended certificate as to the practicability of supplying the proposed office with mail.

Very respectfully,

J. P. Burslow

Fourth Assistant Postmaster General.

To Mr. _____

care of the Postmaster of _____, who will please forward to him.

STATEMENT.

The proposed office to be called _Bryant, Ind Ter._

Notice directions for selecting post office names on next page.

It will be situated in the _S W_ quarter of Section _29_, Township _11_ (North or South).
Range _12_ (East or West), in the County of _Creek Nation_, State of _Indian Terr_.
It will be on or near route No. _St. L. & S. F. RR_, being the route from _Denison Tex_
to _Sapulpa Ind Ter_, on which the mail is now carried _4_ times per _day_.
Will it be directly on this route?—Ans. _yes_
If not, how much would its supply on this route increase the distance necessarily traveled by the carrier in going once over the route?
If not on any route and a "Special Office" is wanted, from what office to be supplied?
The name of the nearest office to the proposed one, on one side, is _Nuyaka S. T._
its distance is _8_ miles in a _Southerly_ direction from the proposed office.
The name of the nearest office, on the other side, is _Henryetta S T_
its distance is _8_ miles in a _Northerly_ direction from the proposed office.
The name of the other nearest office to the proposed one is _Sand Ind. S T_
its distance by the most direct road is _about 8_ miles in a _Easterly_ direction from the proposed office.
The name of the most prominent river near it is _North Canadian_
The name of the nearest creek is _Bad Creek_
The proposed office will be _about 4_ miles from said river, on the _North_
side of it, and will be _about 1_ miles from said nearest creek, on the _North East_ side of it.
The name of the nearest railroad is _St. L. & S. F. RR_
If on the line of or near a railroad, on which side will the office be located; how far from the track; and what is, or will be, the name of the station?—Ans. _North Side about 800 yds. at Bryant Station_
Give the population to be supplied by the proposed office.—Ans. _about 40 families_
If it be a village, state the number of inhabitants.—Ans.
A diagram, or sketch from a map, showing the position of the proposed new office, with neighboring river or creek, roads, and other post offices, towns, or villages near it, will be useful, and is therefore desired.
ALL WHICH I CERTIFY to be correct and true, according to the best of my knowledge and belief, this _____
day of _Sept 24_ 190 _4_
(Sign full name.) _G. Halick, Burroughs_ Proposed P. M.
I CERTIFY that I have examined the foregoing statement, and that it is correct and true, to the best of my knowledge and belief.
(This must be signed by Postmaster at nearest office.)

Alvin W Meacham
Postmaster at _Henryetta IT_
Dist _6_

(OVER.)

_1 63 00 f_

Diagram showing the site of the _____ Bryant _____ Post Office, in Township _11_ (N. or S.), Range _12_ (E. or W.) of _____ I _____ Principal Meridian, County of _____ Creek Nation _____, State of _____ Indian Terry _____, with the adjacent Townships and Post Offices.

It is requested that the exact site of the proposed or existing Post Office, as also the roads to the adjoining offices, and the larger streams or rivers, be marked on this diagram, to be returned as soon as possible to the Post Office Department.

(NORTH.)

(SOUTH.)

Scale one-third inch to the mile.

Establishment of Postal service at Bryant – Page 2
September 24, 1904

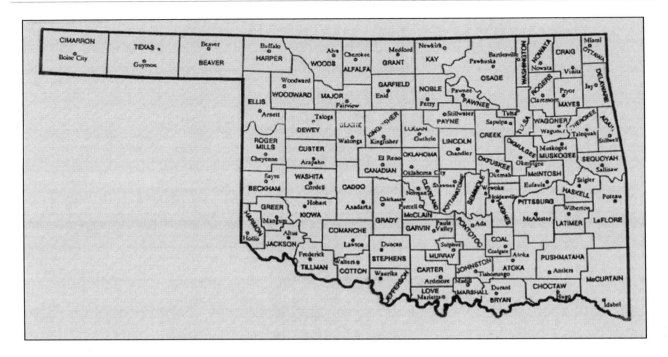

COUNTIES WERE CREATED WHEN OKLAHOMA BECAME THE 46TH STATE OF THE UNION ON NOVEMBER 16, 1907

BOTTOM LEFT: After statehood, the former Creek Nation ended up as parts of Rogers, Mayes, Creek, Tulsa, Wagoner, Cherokee, Okmulgee, Muskogee, Okfuskee, McIntosh, Seminole, and Hughes Counties.

BOTTOM RIGHT: Map of Okmulgee County, showing the location of the Town of Bryant. Bryant is in the southwestern part of the county, southwest of Henryetta.

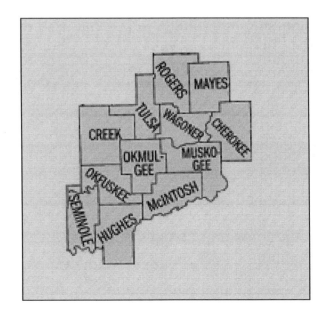

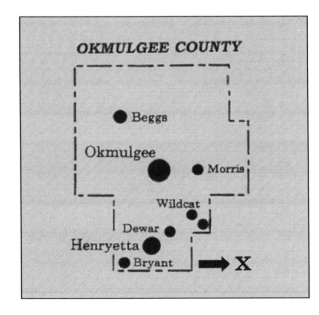

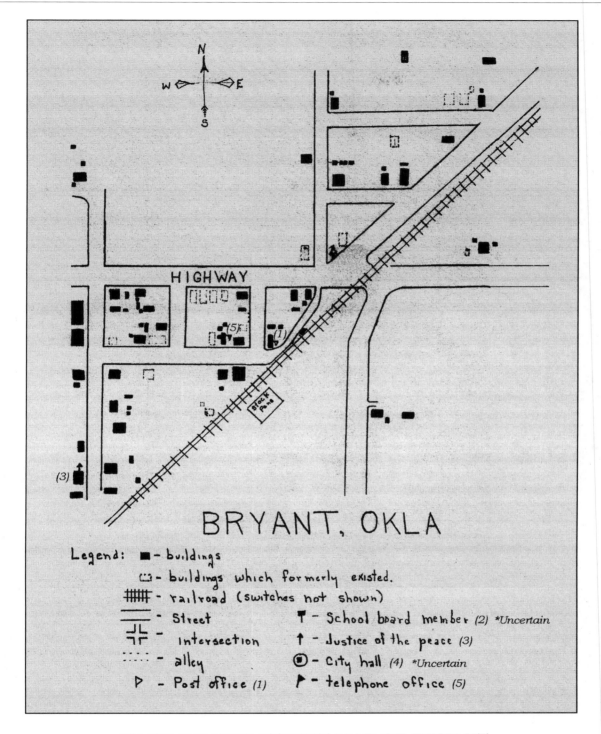

HAND-DRAWN STREET MAP OF BRYANT
(Exact Date Unknown)

Note that this map was hand-drawn from memory. It was not drawn to scale, no street names are shown, and the legend is incomplete and imprecise. Even back when it was made, some of the early buildings of Bryant had been gone for many years. Only approximate locations could be remembered. Note, too, that civic services were located in different buildings at different times.

DOWNTOWN BRYANT, OKLAHOMA
IN THE 1920'S

J. M. Herrin's General Mercantile Company, a Chesterfield Cigarettes sign, the Blue Front Cafe, the Good Eats Cafe, Ray's Garage, City Tailor Shop, Mack's Cafe, the Chile Parlor Cafe, and the Bryant Mercantile Company & Feed Store. The building at the top right center (with the spire) is the Bryant Elementary School and the building directly to the right of the Elementary School (barely visible) is Bryant High School.

SOURCE: Courtesy of the Henryetta Historical Society.

Henry Lee Chancey, standing in front of the Bryant Mercantile Store or, simply, Chancey's Store, in 1933. At one time, this store was owned by Henry Harwell.

BUSINESSES AT BRYANT — AROUND 1940

The building at the left is the Curtis Market, in which the Bryant Post Office and the Bryant Telephone Exchange as well as the Curtis home were located. The Post Office and Telephone Exchange were at the front of the building; the Curtis family lived in a home that was attached to the back of the store. The large rock building at the right was, at the time, Almerigi's Groceries, Drugs & Sundries, and the smaller building directly in front of Almerigi's is Henry Lee Chancey's Bryant Mercantile Store.

Locals referred to the larger building as "The Old Rock Store." It was a very nice store at one time, at which clothing and sundries and other items were sold. Some say that it was owned by Erin (spelling uncertain) Chancey before it was bought by the Almerigi's. After that, it was referred to as "Almerigi's Store." When the building was abandoned in later years, it finally collapsed in place. At that point local people hauled away as much rock and usable building materials as could be salvaged. Today, it is impossible to tell even as much as where the building once stood. Many of the old stores and buildings of Bryant met the same fate.

THE CURTIS MARKET AT BRYANT — AROUND 1940

This building housed the Curtis Market, in which both the Bryant Post Office and the Bryant Telephone Exchange were located for a while. The Post Office and Telephone Exchange were located at the front of the store; the Curtis family home was attached to the back of the store.

MYRNA, BILLY, AND BETTY CURTIS

DELORIS POPEJOY AND CLAE CURTIS
AROUND 1951

They are standing at the back of the building in which the Bryant Post Office, the Bryant Telephone Exchange, the Curtis Grocery Store, and the Curtis family home were located. They are, in other words, at the back entry of the Curtis family's home.

FRISCO BELL AND DELORIS POPEJOY
AROUND 1951

They are standing in front of an old two-story house that once existed in Bryant. Note that this particular house was not the Curtis family home or the Curtis Store or the post office.

MARY LUE CURTIS, BASKETBALL QUEEN OF 1953

Mary Lue, in formal dress, is standing in front of the building in which the Bryant Post Office (on west side), the Telephone Exchange (on east side), and the Curtis home (which was behind the Post Office and Telephone Exchange, at the back of the building) used to be housed. By this date, the Curtis Market, which at one time was also located in this same building, was no longer in operation.

LEFT

Minerva Curtis

RIGHT

Mary Lue Curtis

CHAPTER 8

BRYANT PUBLIC SCHOOL

Bryant's promoters and civic leaders were well aware of how important the availability of schooling was to their own future success, thus they were interested from the beginning in getting a school constructed and in doing whatever they could to make sure it not only succeeded but prospered. Families weren't likely to settle at a town site unless they were sure that schooling would be available for their children, so it made good business sense for them to be of that mind. There's no doubt about it: Access to good schooling was one of the key ways that budding Indian Territory town sites competed against each another for settlers during the early 1900's.

There were plenty of problems to contend with in the Territory in those days, but in some ways the area really wasn't as wild and wooly as was often made out to be. For example, even though Indian families were in the majority at the time, they had leaders who believed in and valued education. Many of the Creeks of the Bryant area had once been residents of South Carolina, where they had learned to speak English before being relocated to Oklahoma. Some of the Anglo students who arrived in the area were surprised to learn that there were Creek students at Bryant who could read and write as well as they could.

The earliest school that served children of the Anglos settlers of Bryant was built in 1901 as part of the land agreement made between Creek Indian allotment land owner Joshua Asbury and Logan Harper, a local school teacher. As one of the early proponents of starting not only a town but also a school at Bryant, Harper had encouraged Asbury to donate enough of his land for both. Asbury agreed, and, later on, once the town was laid out and the first school building was in place, Harper became its first schoolmaster. Both the town and school were in operation years before Bryant became a township and Oklahoma became a State of the Union.

According to Homer Chancey and other long-term residents of the area, the first school was a small three-room wood frame structure, a building that played a dual role as a church on Sundays. It was operated on a subscription basis (i.e., parents paid fees), since support allowances for public schools did not become available until after Oklahoma gained statehood in 1907. After statehood, boundaries drawn up by Henry Lee Chancey defined the school district as extending three miles north and three and one-half miles east of the town site. The first board members of the new Bryant School were Henry Lee Chancey,

Frank Bonar, and Phillip Smith, and one of the earliest teachers hired was a Miss Tolby, who taught all the grade levels that were offered—grades one through eight. As the school grew, more teachers were added. All the children of Bryant, Indian and white alike, attended the school, along with others who traveled in from the surrounding area.

When it became clear that a larger building would be needed to accommodate the growing number of school-aged children of new families that were moving into the area, bonds were sold to raise funds for the construction of a bigger and better school. Using funds raised by means of the bond sale, a new two-story brick grammar school building was constructed and placed in service at the beginning of the 1912-1913 academic year. A man by the name of J. D. Ross was one of those who helped build it. By this time, five teachers were employed by the school, and enrollment had climbed to around 300 students. In later years, as many as 400 students attended school at Bryant.

The new building had classrooms on the second floor as well as an auditorium, which, as was the case for the previous building, served double duty as a church on Sundays. The building featured a coal burning basement furnace to produce steam that was circulated through pipes to radiators that heated the various rooms. A bell mounted in a tower located at the very center of the building was rung at the start of every day. It could be heard for miles around.

When it was determined after the new building was finished that lamps were needed to better illuminate the auditorium, girls who attended the school organized a club for the purpose of raising money. After piecing together a quilt

Cora Barker

and making pies that could be sold, they organized a *pie supper* at which the pies could be auctioned off. Bids were taken for the quilt, which was presented after it was sold to the girl who was voted to be the *the prettiest in Bryant*. The winner was a girl by the name of Cora Barker. The money raised by the girls was used to buy hanging kerosene lamps that were placed around the auditorium. The girls were proud of their lamps, which were described by teachers and residents of the community as being *very pretty*. Somehow or another, later on yet another item was secured for use in the auditorium--a piano. It was used by the school and church alike.

A man by the name of Earl Shepard served as principal during this period of time, and when he left he was replaced by E. P. Baldwin. Among the teachers during these years were Mrs. Orendorf, Mrs. Nettie Godwin, Elmer Heard, as well as the two principals, Mr. Shepard, Mr. Baldwin. Mr. Shepard was known for starting class off every morning by having students sing his favorite hymn, *Lead Kindly*

Light. Among the students who graduated from the school shortly thereafter were Gene, Roy, and Grace Chancey, Anna Price, Cleo Murray, and Belle Ross. There were, of course, other graduates, whose names are unknown.

As larger eighth grade classes began to graduate during the following years, it became clear that there were enough older students in the area to warrant the construction of a high school. At this point, graduation requirements were raised to twelve years and yet another school was brought on line—this time a new brick high school that was placed in service in 1922. The new Bryant High School was built beside the existing Bryant Elementary School.

It was not unusual in those times for students to be older before they finished school, since many of them had to drop in and out repeatedly to help on family farms. This led to some students being well up in age before they finally graduated. Gene Chancey, for example, was 25 years old when he graduated from Bryant High School. Also, former students Belle Ross and Sid Hunter were married in the same auditorium of the brick two-story grade school building in which their grade school graduation ceremony had been held.

Basketball was as popular as a sport back then as it is today, but at most rural schools of the times students played the game using rings put up on dirt courts located just outside their school buildings. Gene Chancey was one of many students who recalled very well and wrote about having played the game outside on one of those dirt courts. Years later, after graduating from Bryant High School at the age of 25 and eventually becoming a member of the Bryant School Board, he and another board member, Ben Furr, traveled to a bank in nearby Weleetka to arrange a loan for the purpose of constructing a gymnasium on the school campus. Using wood framing and covering of sheet iron, they built the first gymnasium at Bryant School. It, too, just like the old outdoor court, had a dirt floor, but afterwards the school had a very good basketball team.

At the time, Chancey operated the Bryant Post Office out of a combination grocery store and meat market he owned, a business that was located within easy walking distance from the school. (He slept, by the way, at least for a while, in a lean-to that was attached to the side of the store building.) At noon he offered lunches to students and others who stopped by to sit at a table he set up for customers. A common lunch bought off his shelves in those days was a tin of salmon or sardines that people would eat as they sat in the store. When school turned out in the afternoon, other groups would stop by the store to pick up family mail.

During the Thirties when the Roosevelt Administration's Works Progress Administration (or WPA) was in full swing in terms of launching efforts designed to help municipalities deal with the effects of the Great Depression, a number of these projects were implemented at Bryant School. During the 1937-38 school year when Myron Oates was Superintendent of Schools, the auditorium, all classrooms, and the gymnasium were painted; sidewalks were put in; the school grounds were improved; and a number of other projects were completed. In addition, a small lunchroom was built on campus, a place where good hamburgers could be bought for five cents each.

When the hard times of the 1930's and 1940's didn't let up and led to a severe decline in the local population, Bryant High School finally had to be shut down. When its doors were closed at the end of the 1957 school year, students were directed to attend high school in nearby Weleetka. Then, around two years later, Bryant Elementary School suffered the same fate. At that point, children of families that remained in the area were redirected to attend school at Henryetta, Weleetka, or Graham. Needless to say, closing the schools was pretty much the final nail in the coffin, as far as the Town of Bryant was concerned.

After many years, the two brick school buildings as well as the gymnasium that was attached to the high school deteriorated into ruins. At least for a while, people lived in one of the buildings; whether they were renters or squatters is unknown. After the buildings started to collapse and become a danger, they were bought by Homer Chancey, who had them torn down. Today, the site where the buildings once stood is so covered by shrubs, brush, and trees that it is all but impossible to tell that they were ever there. There's no doubt about it; the buildings came to a sad end, at least for those who have fond memories of having attended school or taught there at one time.

Among the many teachers and administrators who were once employed by one or the other of the two schools at Bryant were Aubrey Allen, Mrs. Aubrey Allen, Mr. Bailey, E. P. Baldwin, Miss Baldwin, Laura Bernard, Thresie Berta, Miss Brookes, Joe Burnett, John Burns, Mr. Canifax, Jean Cannavan, M. L. Carder, Miss Carpenter, Irish Carter, Ardena Chancey, Oneta Chancey, Opal Chancey, Ruth (Kennedy) Chancey, Sibyl (Jones) Chancey, Vera (Ross) Chancey, George Collins, Mabel Cox, Helen (French) Furr, Juanita (Furr) Inglish, Manual "Mannie" John Furr, Adina George, Mr. Gibble, Nettie Goodwin, Floye Graham, Roland Hardin, Logan Harper, Elmer Heard, Lloyd Hutchison, Mr. Littlefield, Mr. Johns, Opaline Manes, Everett Manns, Fern Maylen, Miss McKinney, Christine (Combest) Milsap, Charlie Minyard, Mr. Moore, J. Myron Oates, Mrs. J. M. Oates, Veta (Porter) Oates, Mrs. Orendorf, Mrs. Peters, Earl Pippin, Milton Ramey, Cecil Riddle, Joe Riddle, Mr. Roper, Eunice Rowe, Miss Marie Samples, Miss Sanders, John D. Seals, Mrs. John D. Seals, T. J. Sexton, Earl Shepard, Hazel Sparks, Mrs. Tolby, Ralph Trousdale, Mr. Vernon, Beulah Vaughn, R. E. Wilson, and Ruby E. Wilson. Several points should be noted with regard to this listing. First, the list is definitely not exhaustive. Second, the names are in alphabetical order rather than order of service. Finally, a good number of the individuals who are named held down dual roles at the school, either as superintendent, principal, coach, bus driver, or board member.

It would be difficult if not impossible to name all the children who attended school at Bryant at one time or another, but a good number of them are pictured in the pages that follow. Looking at their pictures provides a reminder of the fact that there really was a time when Bryant School was a vital and thriving place!

PRINCIPALS/ SUPERINTENDENTS OF BRYANT SCHOOL		
NAME	FROM	TO
Logan Harper	1901	1902
Irish Carter	1907	1908
Roland Hardin	1908	1909
Elmer Heard	1909	1910
Mr. Moore	1911	1912
E. P. Baldwin	1912	1913
Mr. Johns	1913	1914
M. L. Carder	1914	1915
Milton Ramey	1915	1916
John Burns	1922	1923
Mr. Canafax	1924	1925
Cecil Riddle	1925	1926
Mr. Vernon	1926	1927
John Seals	1927	1928
Joe Riddle	1929	1930
Mr. Bailey	1930	1931
Joe Burnett	1931	1937
Myron Oates	1937	1942
Ronald. E. Wilson	1942	1943
Aubrey R. Allen	1944	1946
Earl Pippin	1947	1950
Charles "Charlie" Minyard	1951	1955
Everett Manns	1956	1958
Jess Short	1958	1960

NOTE: Many names as well as exact terms of service are unknown. The dates that are given are only approximate.

WOOD FRAME
BRYANT ELEMENTARY SCHOOL BUILDING OF 1901
During the early years of the town site, this three-room building
served as Bryant's subscription school during the week and as
a church building on Sundays.

THE BRICK TWO-STORY
BRYANT ELEMENTARY SCHOOL OF 1912

THE BRICK TWO-STORY
BRYANT ELEMENTARY SCHOOL OF 1912

These pictures were taken in 1921. At one time, over 400 students were enrolled and the school employed six or more teachers.

A CLASS PICTURE FROM 1921

Front Row — Loren Cole, Harry Hardin, Bobby Dolina, Manual Furr, and James Williamson; Second Row — Albert Chancey, Lee Hammer, James Furr, Gus _____, Haskell Chancey, Darrel Martin, James Bell, Haskell Brown, and Teacher Miss Sanders (sitting on the step at the right); Third Row — Leona Trover, Mamie Le'Gard, Margaret Steffler, Unknown, Clarice Wimberly, Anna Steffler, and Norma West; and Top (Back) Row — Vera Almerigi, Irene Young, Nona Hunter, Jewell Zellner, Oma Hunter, Margaret Bister, and Lora Brannon.

NOTE: The teacher may be misidentified.

STUDENTS
VERA ALMERIGI
AND
LEE HAMMER
IN 1921

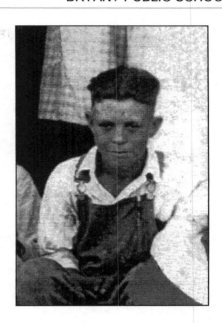

THE BRICK BRYANT HIGH SCHOOL OF 1922

The building at the right is the Bryant High School that was constructed in 1922. The Bryant Elementary School of 1912 is at the left. This photograph was taken from a garden in the back yard of the family home of Pete Salvino, his daughter Margaret Cathcart, and his grand daughter Mary (Cathcart) Campbell. Their home was located directly across the street from the school.

A class during the 1928-29 school year, names unknown.
The teacher is T. J. Sexton.

Teacher
T. J. Sexton

GIRLS BASKETBALL TEAM OF 1928
Ann Karp, Alice Ayers, Sibyl Jones (later Sibyl Chancey), Marie Sluss, "Cotton" Wilkie, Susie West, Hallie Martin, Alice Wilkie, and Ardena Chancey

BOYS BASKETBALL TEAM OF 1929
Kneeling – Ralph Kennedy, Jim Wickersham, Basil Freedel, and Lyle Kennedy; Standing – Dale George, Ike Taylor, and Jack Furr

TEACHING STAFF FROM 1927 TO 1929
Miss Laura Benard, Mrs. John Seals, Mr. John D. Seals, T. J.
Sexton, Miss Marie Samples, and Miss Carpenter. Not pictured are
Mr. Gibble and Miss Adina George.

CLASS OF 1929
Leona Trover and Dale George. There probably were more
graduates this year, but no picture of the graduating class could be
found.

HOME ECONOMICS CLASS OF 1930
Alice Wilkie (sitting), "Tencie" Mainard, Olenice Anderson (far back), Faye Lewis, Edith Wickersham (sitting), Ema Cain, Sibyl Jones, Laura Benard, Hallie Martin (back), Oneta Chancey (sitting), and teacher Mrs. T. A. Anderson (far right).

TEACHER-COACH JOE RIDDLE AND
TEACHER MARIE SAMPLES — AROUND 1930

BOYS BASKETBALL TEAM OF 1930
David Almerigi, Henry Chancey, Homer Horner, Joe Riddle (Superintendent and Coach), Earl McCain, Fay Wheeler, and Bill Furr.

GIRLS BASKETBALL TEAM OF 1930
Johnie Mainard, Ardena Chancey, "Tensie" Mainard, Hallie Martin, Alice Wilkie, Gladys Wilkie, Alice Ayers, Sibyl Jones, and Susie West. Coach Joe Riddle also served as teacher and superintendent.

CLASS OF 1930
"Teencie" Mainard, Hallie Martin, Alice Wilkie, Jim Wickersham, Olinse Anderson, Sibyl Jones, and Edith Wickersham.   Graduate Sibyl Jones (later Sibyl Chancey) is enlarged below.

Teacher
Mrs. T. A. Anderson
and
Graduate
Sybil Jones

CLASS OF 1934
Standing – Faye Lewis, Bill Furr, Homer Horner, Ardena Chancey, and Nugent Dodge; Sitting - Mildred Hunter, Vivian (Duke) Ross, & Billy Milam.

CLASS OF 1940
Front – Mrs. J. M. Oates, Kenneth Harris, Delmis Sluss, Dorothy DeVoe, and Superintendent J. M. Oates; Back – Orville Henley, Norman Chancey, Victor Struckle, Raymond Christenberry, Leona McCrory, & Leonard Davis.

ELEMENTARY SCHOOL PHOTO IN 1937
NAMES UNKNOWN

TEACHER
LLOYD HUTCHISON

STUDENT
TED CHANCEY

CLASS OF 1941

Front Row – Uncertain, Uncertain, and Pauline Birdcreek; Back Row – Tom Fowler, Uncertain, Judson McKelvey, Uncertain, Teddy Chancey, Class Sponsor Mrs. Veta (Porter) Oates, and Uncertain. Note that some of the names are, as stated, uncertain or unknown, and others may be out of order.

NOTE: The 11 seniors of the Class of 1941 were Herman Bell, Pauline Birdcreek, Edna Mae Buchanan, Teddy Chancey, John Farley, Tom Fowler, Travis Huckabay, Judson McKelvey, Catherine Ramay, Juanita Thompson, and Cleo Thomason. One student is missing from the picture.

FOOTBALL TEAM OF 1940-41

Kneeling – Bob Baily, Virgil Jackson, Tom "Jelly" Fowler, Unknown, Jack Wallace, and Cecil "Baldy" Sluss. Standing – Coach J. M. Oates, Ted "Bryant" Lowe, "Chubby" or "Tubby" or "Chub," Billy "Buck" Buchanan, Douglas James, Travis Huckaby, Ted "Sweet Potatoes" Chancey, Carthol Phillips, Winford "Windy" Chancey, Bill Reed, Eldon Guinn, and an Assistant Coach (Name Unknown).

GROUP OF STUDENTS – 1940-41 SCHOOL YEAR

Teacher Juanita (Inglish) Furr is at the far right, marked by an X. Other names unknown. Billy Furr is seated in the front row, also marked with an X.

FIRST, SECOND, AND THIRD GRADES IN 1940-41
THE TEACHER IS ONETA CHANCEY.

TEACHER
ONETA CHANCEY

STUDENT
DONALD DANIEL

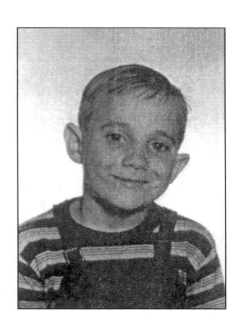

SENIOR PLAY OF 1940-41

Playcast of "That Watkins Girl": Ted Chancey, Tom Fowler, Catherine Ramey, Judson McKelvey, Juanita Robinson, Lois McClain, Edna Mae Buchanan, John Farley, and Director Veta (Porter) Oates. Student names are not in order. At bottom, Teacher-Director Veta (Porter) Oates and student Ramona Cowan.

CLASS OF 1942

Front – Mrs. J. M. Oates, Bennie Hardin, Jerry Davis, Lucille Farley, Harold Richardson, and Frances Brown. Back – Raymond Stevenson, Winford R. Francis "Red" Chancey, Teddy Lowe, Carthol Phillips, and J. M. Oates, Superintendent. At bottom, Teacher J. M. Oates and student Juanita Middleton.

MARTHA BELLE DAVIS — CLASS OF 1944

*NOTE: There may have been more graduates this
year, but no picture of them could be found.*

CLASS OF 1945
Beth Pippin (left) and Bertha Ryal

JUNIORS AND SENIORS OF 1944-45
BACK: Senior Guandina Elizabeth Pippin, Teacher Ruby E. Wilson, Senior Bertha Ryal, and Junior Marie Cleland. FRONT: Junior Jimmy Curtis, Junior Lorene Tabor, Junior Louise Daniel, and Junior Carlie Curtis.

BRYANT SCHOOL PHOTOGRAPH IN 1947

FRONT ROW: Dudley Hardin (sitting), Claudine Hardin (checked dress), June Evelyn Curtis, Bobby James, Barbara Wasson, Brunell Sanford, Betty Turner, and Carl Gene Daniel.   SECOND ROW: Tommy Roberts (standing, thumb in pants pocket), Jimmy Smith, Thelma Davis, Naomi Roberts, Gertrude Williams, Christine Birdcreek, Deloris Popejoy, and Dawson Popejoy.   THIRD ROW: George Brison, Bobby Dodson, Delores Pippin. Maxine Crawford, and Teacher Opaline Manes. BACK ROW: Gerald Sanford, Durward Chancey, Roy Bardin, Teacher Charlie Minyard, Dee Massey, Dorothie James, Lou Jo Minyard, Kenneth Popejoy, Dwight Wasson, and Superintendent A. R. Allen.

CLASS OF 1947

Dee Massey, Delores Pippin, Deloris Popejoy, Superintendent-Teacher-Coach Aubrey Allen, Doris Popejoy, Maxine Crawford, Naomi Roberts, and Dawson Popejoy. At bottom are teachers Mr. and Mrs. Aubrey Allen.

THE POPEJOY TRIPLETS OF THE CLASS OF 1947

Deloris (Left), Dawson, and Doris Popejoy

FRESHMEN THELMA DAVIS, BARBARA WASSON,
AND JUNE EVELYN CURTIS IN 1946

FIRST BRYANT SCHOOL GYMNASIUM — AROUND 1948

This wood frame tin-sided building is the first Bryant School Gymnasium. At least for a time, it had a dirt floor. The exact year it was constructed is uncertain. When this gymnasium was destroyed by fire (year unknown), it was replaced by a new brick gymnasium that extended out from the back of the high school. The small white house at the left is the home of Opaline Manes, a high school commerce teacher who got around by using a wheelchair. Mary (Cathcart) Campbell is standing in the snow at the right side of the gym.

BASKETBALL PLAYERS — DECEMBER, 1948

*Barbara Wasson, Dorothie James, Christine Birdcreek, and Janevelyn
Curtis. They are standing in front of the first Bryant School Gymnasium.*

BRYANT ELEMENTARY SCHOOL,
AFTER THE TOP FLOOR WAS REMOVED

When it was discovered that the Elementary School needed extensive repairs, the building was remodeled and the top story was removed. At that time, enrollment had already begun to decline. The stark white building behind the school is the old wood-frame tin-sided gymnasium. The smaller white building at the far left was the home of Commerce Teacher Opaline Manes. At bottom are teacher Opaline Manes and student Dorothie James.

CLASS OF 1949

Gerald Sanford (top left), Roy Bardin (top center), Dwight Wasson (right), Gladys Klimek (left), & Dorothie James (right).

BELOW

Charlene Hardin with Junevelyn and Mary Lou Curtis in 1949

CLASS OF 1950

Teacher Charlie Minyard, Jack Reddick, Junevelyn Curtis, Barbara Wasson, Claudene Hardin, Durward Chancey, Jimmie Smith, and Betty Turner

Sue (left) and Gerene Good

CLASS OF 1951

Gary Muehlhausen, Charlene Minyard, Dudley Hardin, George Brison, Christine Birdcreek, and Bobby James

GRADE SCHOOL STUDENTS IN 1951-52

Virgie Sanders (in the front row in the middle) and her twin brother Virgil Sanders (to her right in the dark coveralls). Their brother "Bunny" is in the back row, the first child opposite Teacher Sibyl Chancey

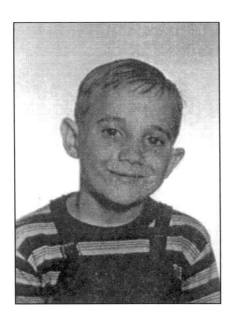

Don and Billie Lois Daniel

*PLAYMATES LINDA DANIEL, VIRGIE SANDERS,
AND CONNIE DAVIS IN 1953*

CLASS OF 1952

Ramona Cowan, Juanita Middleton, Jacklyn Chancey, Melvin Reddick, Teacher-Superintendent Aubrey Allen, Coy Anglin, and Joe Jack Struckle.

NOTE: At the end of a career of over 25 years in education during which he held positions as Teacher, Dean of Students, Associate Professor of Education, and, finally, President of Northwestern Oklahoma State University at Alva, Dr. Joe J. Struckle of the Bryant High School Class of 1952 was honored by his employer when a building was named after him. (See "Reunions" Chapter)

Joe Jack Struckle
Class of 1952

Ramona Cowan
Class of 1952

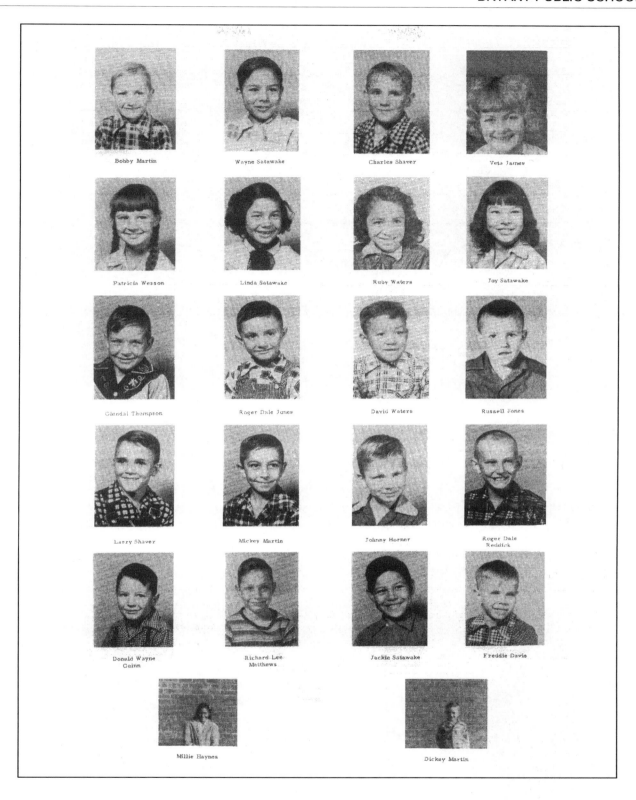

Bobby Martin   Wayne Satawake   Charles Shaver   Veta James

Patricia Wesson   Linda Satawake   Ruby Waters   Joy Satawake

Glendal Thompson   Roger Dale Jones   David Waters   Russell Jones

Larry Shaver   Mickey Martin   Johnny Horner   Roger Dale Reddick

Donald Wayne Guinn   Richard Lee Matthews   Jackie Satawake   Freddie Davis

Millie Haynes   Dickey Martin

ELEMENTARY SCHOOL STUDENTS
1952-53 SCHOOL YEAR

CLASS OF 1953

Gerald Graham, Don Lee, Robert Sutterfield, Dane Lee, Eziel John Harjo, Henry Barrett, Mary Lue Curtis, Barbara Shirleen Reddick, Patsy Ruth Turner, and Teacher Charles Minyard. At bottom, Teachers Charles Minyard and Sibyl Chancey.

GIRLS BASKETBALL TEAM OF 1952-53
Top Row: Patsy Turner, Geraldine Minyard, Myrtle Birdcreek, Ruth Kub,
Joann Dodson, and Phyllis Graham; Bottom Row: Mary Curtis, Barbara
Reddick, Coach Charlie Minyard, Billie Sue Minyard, and Billie Lois Daniel

GIRLS BASKETBALL TEAM of 1953-54
Kneeling: Betty Faye Curtis, Earlene Good, Virginia James, Gerene Good,
and Linda Kay Minyard. Back Row: Billy Lois Daniel, Betty Ann Allen,
Billye Sue Minyard, Ruth Kub, Geraldine Minyard, Patsy Jean Allen, and
Teacher Charley Minyard.

CLASS OF 1954

Top Row – Wilma Sutterfield, Joe Hardin, and Sue Daniel. Middle Row – Leona Riley, Betty Emery, and Myrtle Birdcreek. Bottom Row – Wanda Horner, Joann James, and Billy Taber

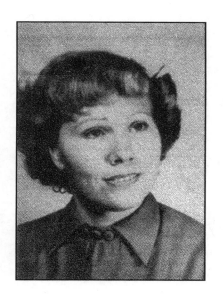

BRYANT SCHOOL
CLASS OF 1955

Top Row – Lois Coleman, Billy Curtis, and Betty Curtis. Bottom Row – Virginia James, Norma Thomas, and Ruth Kub.

BRYANT SCHOOL
CLASS OF 1956

Top Row – Billie Daniel, Phyllis Graham, and Jackie Pippin. Middle Row – Myrtle Birdcreek and Wesley Asbury. Bottom Row – Jimmie Wasson, Bobby Pippin, and Donald Choate

BRYANT SCHOOL CLASS OF 1957

Lue Haynes, Mona Guinn, Larry David, and Earl Freeman

NOTE: Last class to graduate from Bryant High School

SOME BRYANT SCHOOL TEACHERS
AND ADMINISTRATORS THROUGH THE YEARS

Teacher
Mrs. T. A. Anderson

Teacher-Coach
Joe Riddle

Teacher
Manual John Furr

Teacher
John D. Seals

Teacher
Mrs. John D. Seals

*Teacher
Ruby E. Wilson*

*Principal
R. E. Wilson*

*Teacher
Mabel Cox*

*Superintendent
Aubrey Allen*

*Teacher
Hazel Sparks*

*Dietician Mrs.
Aubrey Allen*

Teacher
Opaline Manes

Teacher
Eunice Rowe

Principal
Jean Cannavan

Teacher
Floye Graham

Principal
Everett Manns

Principal
Charles Minyard

Teacher
Beulah Vaughn

Teacher
Sybil Chancey

Teacher
Opal Chancey

Teacher
Juanita (Furr) Inglish

Teacher
Marie Samples

Principal
Fern Maylen

Principal
George R. Collins

Teacher
Laura Bernard

Teacher
T. J. Sexton

Teacher
Oneta Chancey

Teacher
Lloyd Hutchison

Teacher
Mrs. Carpenter

*Teacher Veta
(Porter) Oates*

*Superintendent
J. M. Oates*

*Teacher
Thresie Berta*

*Teacher
Ardena Chancey*

*Teacher
Miss Sanders*

*Principal
Ralph Trousdale*

*TWO VIEWS OF BRYANT HIGH SCHOOL
AROUND 1945 – EXACT YEARS UNKNOWN*

*NOTE: The extension behind the building at the
bottom is the second gymnasium.*

SOME BRYANT SCHOOL BOARD MEMBERS
OVER THE YEARS

Joe Asbury

Homer Horner

John Cox

George D. Reddick

Gene
Dunson

Lawrence
Muehlhausen

Earl
Pippin

FRONT OF BRYANT HIGH SCHOOL
(EXACT DATE UNKNOWN)

A FEW BRYANT SCHOOL SUPPORT STAFF MEMBERS FROM OVER THE YEARS

LEFT

Cook A. A. Hardin

RIGHT

Mrs. Aubrey Allen,
Dietician

BOTTOM

Cooks
Deana West (Left) and
Besssie Curtis (Right)

BRYANT SCHOOL SUPPORT STAFF

*Bus Drivers (Names Unknown), Bus Driver
and Janitor Mr. Pippin, and Cook Deana West*

CHAPTER 9

BRYANT THROUGH THE YEARS

Only a few of the many people who once lived at Bryant are profiled in the pages that follow, and those who do appear are mentioned only because appropriate information about them could be found—articles, interviews, or pictures that helped illustrate what living at the town site was like on a day-to-day basis. It should also be pointed out that many individuals and families that, due to the significant role they played in the development of the town, really ought to have been included but are not. These folks weren't omitted by design; they were left out only because information about them could not be located. Hopefully, this problem will be remedied by the time this book is updated—a process, by the way, that is already underway.

Among the individuals, families, and businesses that are mentioned are a few who were prosperous according to the standards of the times, but most of them, at least from an economic standpoint, were pretty much average. Making a living at Bryant would never have been described as easy; many of those who lived there, as a matter of fact, spent a good deal of time up against the wall, financially speaking, struggling just to get by. They weren't alone, either, especially after the economic decline that began in the Thirties rolled around. When times got truly rough, the poorer folks of the area (my own family included) discovered that they had a whole lot of company.

Some of the early property owners at Bryant weren't really interested in putting down long-term roots; they showed up only in hope of making quick profits through *land churning*, or buying and reselling real estate in the short term. A number of people who fell into this category came and went over the years, and some properties at Bryant changed hands several times. In addition, researchers who have examined land transfer records for the early years of some Indian Territory town sites have noted that white trustees appointed by courts to *help* early Indian and Negro land allottees manage their holdings on occasion actually either bought their land from them for a pittance or defrauded them of its true value through other legal but unethical means. In this particular area, quite a bit of skullduggery took place back in the old days.

Among the new arrivals who were true settlers, people interested in putting down roots for the long haul, were Henry Lee and Sarah (Mainard) Chancey, a couple that moved to the Indian Territory from Cecil, Arkansas, in 1901. Henry Lee lived at Holdenville for a while and then moved his family to Bryant, where he

Henry Lee Chancey

landed a job widening the dock for the Frisco Railroad. After that, he helped build part of the Fort Smith Railroad, the rail line between Oklahoma City and Fort Smith. His job was to prepare right-of-way for the laying of track.

Henry Lee Chancey lived at Bryant for the remainder of his life. After starting out in the area as a railroad contractor, he held down a number of other positions before he finally retired. He made his living as a farmer-rancher for a while after working for the railroad company employers, and, at the same time, served for a number of years as President of the Board of Brown's Trading Company of Weleetka and as Postmaster of Bryant.

When he saw a need for a bank at Bryant later on, in 1921 he opened and became President of the First State Bank of Bryant. When the bank had to be closed in 1926, he bought the Bryant Mercantile Store from the man who owned it before him, Henry Harwell. Before he finally retired, Henry Lee Chancey accomplished quite a lot for himself, and, at the same time, he also did quite a lot for the Town of Bryant.

One story Henry Lee Chancey's son Joseph Eugene "Gene" Chancey used to tell about his father had to do with their family's early days at Bryant. The town was *well populated* when they moved there, mostly by men who worked in one or the other of the many coal mines active in the vicinity. According to Gene, a good number of the locals who claimed to be Creek Indians really weren't Creeks at all. They did it, he said, to qualify for allotment land allowances, and, to *prove* that they were Creeks, some of them asked Hugh Henry, a Creek who was very well known in the area, to declare that he was their uncle. In at least some cases, apparently, it worked; some of these claimants were, in fact, awarded allotment land. What Gene said of his father, however, was that he refused to do this himself, telling his sons that to do so would be dishonest.

Another early settler of the area southeast of Henryetta near Bryant was Ben Furr, yet another man who moved to the Indian Territory before statehood. Just like Henry Lee Chancey, he did quite a lot for the Town of Bryant. Ben Furr was a pioneering cattle rancher in the area, but he also took part in many civic activities. His wife was Stella Mae (Miller) Furr, and it is interesting to note that she and Ben were married by Colonel John L.

Ben Furr

Peacock, an early day occupant of the old Creek Council House at Okmulgee. Their wedding ceremony was held in the same aging brick building in which Indian warriors once held pow wows.

Ben Furr was elected county commissioner of his district in 1932 and then re-elected in 1934. He also served on several occasions as a member of the County Excise Board and as a member of the Bryant School Board. He was considered one of the most economically-minded public officials the county ever had. He passed away at an Oklahoma City hospital on September 27, 1961, at the age of 78.

Yet another civic-minded resident of Bryant was Peter Salvino, a man who had an unusual and highly interesting background. He was the first child born in the United States to Italian immigrant parents, Antone and Mary Salvino, who moved to Bryant to work in one of the many mines that were active in the area during the early years of the community. When Pete was born on January 1, 1891, he joined two older brothers who had been born in Italy.

Pete Salvino

After he grew up, Pete enlisted in the Army during World War I and served on active duty in France. When the Battle of Saint-Mihiel was fought in France from September 12 to September 19 in 1918 between the Germany Empire and allies France and the United States, it resulted in a total of over 7,000 casualties and losses—2,000 dead and 5,000 wounded. Among those hurt in the battle was Pete Salvino, who was caught up in a German mustard gas attack. Fortunately, he survived and was able to return to Bryant.

A small thing Pete did after the a war serves to highlight the kind of man he was. While he was on duty in the trenches in France, he was one of many soldiers who received Red Cross gift packages from supportive patriots back in the States. In one package he received was a pair of socks and an encouraging note from the woman who sent it, Mrs. L. A. Koons of Athens, Ohio. Pete kept the note in the Bible he carried with him from 1917 through the end of the war, and then, when he got back home, he looked up Mrs. Koons' address and then, to show how truly appreciative he had been, mailed the note back to her, thanking her for what she had done and suggesting that she might want to keep it as a souvenir.

It is said of Pete that he never complained about anything, and that he continued to work until he was 76 years of age. He never got married, but kept up a large and beautiful garden for as long as he lived at Bryant, giving away most of what he produced to friends and neighbors. He was widely regarded as kind man of high values who did whatever he could for anyone who needed help. Always close to his nieces and nephews, he took in his sister and her daughter, Mary (Cathcart) Campbell, after her husband died when Mary was 10 years old. That's how Mary and her mother ended up living at Bryant.

Earl Pippin

An incident that happened to Mary at the age of 12 while she was growing up at Bryant and living with her Uncle Pete has to do with one of Pete's neighbors, Earl Pippin, who was Superintendent of Schools at Bryant at the time. When her mother asked her to unplug their washing machine after finishing a load of wash, Mary's thumb became stuck in the socket and electricity surged through her when she tugged at the plug to pry it loose. Hearing Mary and her mother's screams as electrical current coursed through Mary's body, Mr. Pippen heard them and ran from next door as fast as he could to help by knocking her hand loose from the wire. Mary and her mother credited him with saving her life. Although her hand was burned, Mary and her mother were thankful that she was alive!

During the Forties, Mary's Uncle Pete served for a time as Treasurer of Bryant Township. When he died on October 13, 1983, at the age of 90, he was fondly remembered by everyone who knew him. By his relatives, he is recalled as a wonderful human being and a dearly loved member of their family.

What needs to be repeated at the conclusion of this chapter is that only a very few of the many people who lived at Bryant and played an important role in the growth and development of the township have been profiled in this book. Again, no one was left out by design, and, hopefully, more information about the people who lived there will be available by the time it is updated—a process that, again, is already underway. Adding more detail of this kind will explain in even more detail how the growth, development, and decline of Bryant played out and in so doing will greatly strengthen the story. More information, in other words, will only improve the already interesting and wonderful story of the old town you have in your hands today!

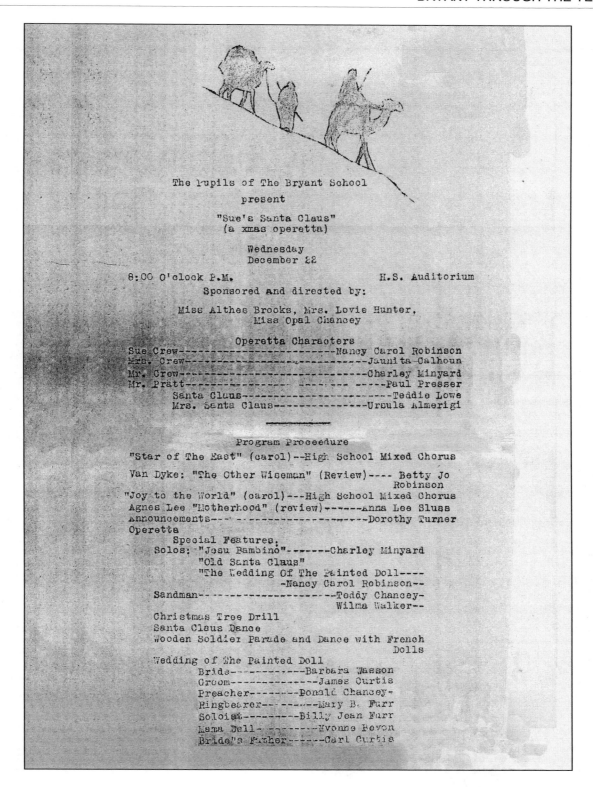

The Pupils of The Bryant School

present

"Sue's Santa Claus"
(a xmas operetta)

Wednesday
December 22

8:00 O'clock P.M.   H.S. Auditorium
Sponsored and directed by:

Miss Althes Brooks, Mrs. Lovie Hunter,
Miss Opal Chancey

Operetta Characters
Sue Crew---------------------------------Nancy Carol Robinson
Mrs. Crew--------------------------------Jaunita Calhoun
Mr. Crew---------------------------------Charley Minyard
Mr. Pratt--------------------- --------- -----Paul Presser
         Santa Claus----------------------Teddie Lowe
         Mrs. Santa Claus-------------Ursula Almerigi

_____

Program Proceedure

"Star of The East" (carol)--High School Mixed Chorus

Van Dyke: "The Other Wiseman" (Review)---- Betty Jo
                                          Robinson
"Joy to the World" (carol)---High School Mixed Chorus
Agnes Lee "Motherhood" (review)-------Anna Lee Sluss
Announcements--- --------------------------Dorothy Turner
Operetta
      Special Features.
      Solos: "Jesu Bambino"-------Charley Minyard
             "Old Santa Claus"
             "The Wedding Of The Painted Doll----
                        -Nancy Carol Robinson--
Sandman---------------------Teddy Chancey-
                           Wilma Walker--
Christmas Tree Drill
Santa Claus Dance
Wooden Soldier Parade and Dance with French
                                      Dolls
Wedding of The Painted Doll
         Bride-------------Barbara Wasson
         Groom---------------James Curtis
         Preacher--------Donald Chancey-
         Ringbearer---------Mary B. Furr
         Soloist---------Billy Jean Furr
         Mama Doll----------Yvonne Bevon
         Bride's Father------Carl Curtis

*A CHRISTMAS OPERETTA FOR THE COMMUNITY
PERFORMED BY PUPILS OF BRYANT SCHOOL
(EXACT DATE UNCERTAIN)*

THE MARVIN AND AMY CHANCEY HOME IN 1912

Marvin's parents were Henry and Sarah (Mainard) Chancey, who were among the earliest white settlers at Bryant. Marvin and Amy's children (pictured below) were Haskell Gore "Red," Herschel Troy, Velma (holding Goldia Elizabeth), and Forest Lee "Cotton" Chancey. One sibling, baby Henry Jackson Chancey (who married Sibyl Jones later on), is not in the photograph.

THE BEN FURR FAMILY — AROUND 1926
Alf Miller "Jack," Albert Clinton, Beatrice, Juanita, mother Stella (Miller), Manual "Manie" or "John" (standing at back), Benjamin Clinton "BC" (on his father's lap), father Benjamin Clinton "Ben" Furr, and Odis Clinton "Bill" Furr

BEN FURR AND SONS — AROUND 1948
STANDING: Alf Miller (3rd son), Albert Clinton (1st son), and Manual "Mannie" or "John" (2nd son). SITTING: Benjamin Clinton "BC" Jr. (5th son), father Benjamin Clinton "Ben," and Odis Clinton "Bill" Furr (4th son)

BEN AND STELLA FURR – AROUND 1955

*Odis Clinton "O. C." or "Bill" Clinton Furr, Stella (Miller)
Furr, Benjamin Clinton Furr, Juanita (Furr) Inglish, Albert
Clinton Furr, and Jack Furr*

GOVERNMENT OF BYRANT TOWNSHIP – AROUND 1944

Pete Salvino (Treasurer), Stanley Davis (Mayor), and Jake Jones (Clerk)

BRYANT EXTENSION HOMEMAKERS
RURAL ROAD SIGN COMMITTEE OF 1944

Jim Holman, Lola Peniquine, Vera Chancey, Co-Chairman of the Sign Committee Maime Sweeney, Homer Chancey, County Commissioner Margie Coleman, Mayor Stanley Davis, President of the Homemakers Dorothy Reddick, Christine Millsap, "Jink" Reddick, Pete Salvino, and Jake Jones.

CHRISTMAS PARTY AT THE HOME OF
TEACHER SIBYL CHANCEY – AROUND 1948

Larry Shaver, Pat Wasson, Wayne Satawake, Unknown, Joy Satawake, Jackie Satawake, Russell Jones, Charles Shaver, Freddy Davis, Donald Guinn, Johnny Guinn, Teacher Sibyl Chancey, Johnny Horner, Linda Satawake, and Rodger Reddick

PAT WASSON AND JACKIE SATAWAKE

HENRY LEE CHANCEY FAMILY IN 1933
Seated – Homer (nicknamed "Hummer" or "Little Pepper"), Marvin Marcellas, Father Henry Lee, Mother Sarah (Mainard), and Albert Martin Chancey. Standing – Roy, Louise (Chancey) Jones, and Joseph Eugene "Gene" Chancey. NOTE: Children Grace and Cleveland are missing, and one child died in infancy

HENRY LEE AND SARAH (MAINARD) CHANCEY IN 1933

EXTENDED FAMILY OF HENRY LEE
AND SARAH (MAINARD) CHANCEY IN 1933

This picture makes it obvious why some have suggested that Bryant really ought to have been called "Chanceyville"!

HENRY LEE CHANCEY

MARVIN AND AMY CHANCEY FAMILY IN 1951

Standing are their children Henry Jackson, Goldia Elizabeth, Herschel Troy, Velma, Haskell Gore "Red," and Forrest Lee "Cotton" Chancey.

FORREST LEE "COTTON" CHANCEY WITH HIS SON MIKE AND DAUGHTER PATRICIA

HAZEL RUTH (KENNEDY) CHANCEY
WITH HER CHILDREN MIKE AND PATRICIA

FOUR GENERATIONS OF CHANCEY MEN
Henry Lee Chancey (left front), Marvin Chancey (right front),
Forrest "Cotton" Chancey (top left), and Mike Chancey

THE HENRY AND SIBYL CHANCEY FAMILY
Henry Jackson and Sibyl (Jones) Chancey and their
daughter Jacklyn and son Durward. Henry's father was
Marvin Chancey, whose father was Henry Lee Chancey.

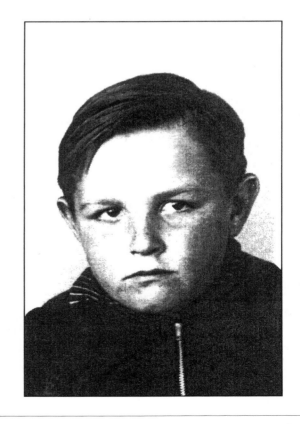

HOMER AND VERA CHANCEY

*Homer, like his father Henry Lee Chancey,
was a long-term resident of Bryant*

MEMBERS OF THE SALVINO FAMILY 1917

Pete Salvino is standing, second from the right.

Pete Salvino and niece Mary Cathcart at his home in Bryant during the Fifties. Bryant School could be seen from the backyard of the Salvino home.

Pete Salvino and has sister Margaret (Salvino) Cathcart
at Pete's home in Bryant.

PETE SALVINO IN HIS GARDEN

FRANK AND BONNIE JAMES
Long-term residents of Bryant

JAMES FAMILY, IN LATER YEARS

James, Don, Frank (at front), Doug, Charlie,
Bobby, Johnny, and Jimmy James

Virginia, Vita Kay, Joann, Dorothie Dean, Nancy,
Maudie (an aunt), and Helen James

FIDDLER CHARLIE JAMES

CHARLIE JAMES

DON JAMES

THE BRYANT COMMUNITY
INTERDENOMINATIONAL CHURCH

The civic entity in addition to Bryant School that deserves special mention in any history of Bryant is the Bryant Community Interdenominational Church. It wasn't launched until the early Fifties, but from that point on it had a notable impact on the lives of many residents of the town and surrounding area. It eventually became known, in fact, as some have put it, Bryant's *place to pray and place to vote.*

B. L. Williams

Christian believers have lived at Bryant since the earliest days of the town site, and, at one time or another over the years, members of at least two or three different denominations tried to establish a fixed presence there. Each one struggled for a while and then eventually fizzled out, mainly because the community was just too small for any one group to reach a critical mass in terms of membership. A Baptist Church, for example, existed at Bryant during the early years of the community, but it didn't last long and very little is known about it today.

The one concern every church group that tried to establish a presence at Bryant had in common was that they had no place to meet except the auditorium of the Bryant Public School. Even with the availability of the school auditorium, however, all through the Forties there were no regular church services held at Bryant. Reverend B. L. Williams and various other lay and student ministers held meetings there on occasion, but no services were offered on a predictable schedule. The lack of regular services at Bryant remained a concern until the early Fifties, when a group of believers decided that something needed to be done about it.

Led by Walter Lynn of nearby Henryetta and John Ford (home town uncertain), it was this group of concerned Christians that launched an initiative to establish a program of regular church services for the Town of Bryant. Further, they decided, the community ought to have a church building of its own, a building that ought to be operated, they believed, given the size of the town, on an interdenominational basis. Although it was something of a stretch for a small group with only $200 in savings to begin thinking along these lines at the time, the members of the group decided to pursue the idea, anyway.

Relying on the promise of funding future members would donate and the availability of volunteer labor offered by their Christian supporters, the group began to do what had to be done to get the project underway. Jake L. Jones, an excellent local carpenter who just happened to be especially interested in seeing a church established at Bryant, put the first major component in place when he volunteered to not only design the church building but also to work with volunteer laborers to do the actual construction. Lumber and other building materials became available when a local lumber company offered to extend credit to the group on highly favorable terms for a loan that the church could make payments on as contributions came in. Then, when Henryettan Lawrence Muehlhausen bought and donated two lots as a site on which the building could be located, all the essentials were in place for the project to begin.

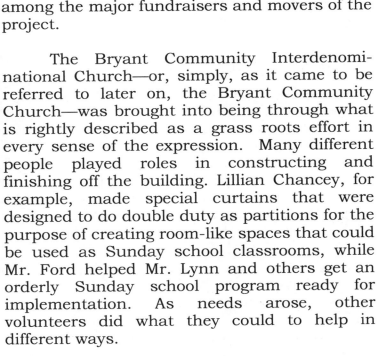

Jake L. Jones

Members of the founding group struggled for years to complete the planning and raise the funding that were required to get their new sanctuary under way. Walter Lynn, for example, devoted many hours to drawing up building plans, completing a church charter, writing operational by-laws, and filing incorporation papers that were required by Oklahoma Secretary of the State. Others, too, contributed many hours of time and labor to help advance the project. Sybil, Opal, Vera, and Lillian Chancey and other women of Bryant were among the major fundraisers and movers of the project.

Lawrence Muehlhausen

The Bryant Community Interdenominational Church—or, simply, as it came to be referred to later on, the Bryant Community Church—was brought into being through what is rightly described as a grass roots effort in every sense of the expression. Many different people played roles in constructing and finishing off the building. Lillian Chancey, for example, made special curtains that were designed to do double duty as partitions for the purpose of creating room-like spaces that could be used as Sunday school classrooms, while Mr. Ford helped Mr. Lynn and others get an orderly Sunday school program ready for implementation. As needs arose, other volunteers did what they could to help in different ways.

When the building was close to completion, a service was scheduled on December 13, 1952, to dedicate the building. The ministers from Henryetta who were on hand to conduct the service were Earl Peters of the Presbyterian Church, W. O. Ferguson of the First Christian Church, R. G. Harris of the First Methodist Church, and W. H. Deitz of the First Nazarene Church. Reverend Peters presided over the session, Reverend Ferguson gave a scripture reading, Reverend Harris delivered a sermon, and Reverend Deitz offered a closing prayer.

When the doors of the new church finally opened on March 7, 1954, it got under way with a total of 19 charter members. Additional members were added during the years that followed. Lynn and Ford also helped plan, schedule, and deliver the first services that were held in the new sanctuary. As a child, I was one of those present for the first service. Various ministers filled the pulpit until early 1955, when Reverend B. L. Williams was hired as the church's first full-time pastor. Through baptismal services that were held at a local farm pond, new members were added to the church during Reverend Williams' term as pastor. In addition, the church building was further enlarged and improved under his leadership when three new classrooms and a concrete walkway were added. During this period of time, a church newsletter called *The Bryant Christian News* was published.

When ill health forced Reverend Williams to retire in September of 1963, he was followed by Mr. John Underwood, a lay minister who became ordained later on. Reverend Underwood served as pastor until February of 1974, when he, too, moved on. Keeping the church alive after his departure until a replacement could be found proved to be a major challenge for the church, since it had such a small membership. Because no pulpit committee was available to handle the task of locating a new pastor, a group composed of members Opal, Homer, and Vera Chancey appointed themselves to get the job done. Vera Chancey, by the way, also served over the years as the congregation's pianist.

The self-appointed search committee scheduled a series of Fifth Sunday Dinners to raise enough funds to keep the church alive until a new full-time pastor could be located, and then began their search in earnest. Among their various efforts to locate new minister was a trip to the neighboring town of Wetumka to visit with a Chancey family member, a cousin who had married a Holiness preacher by the name of Nolan Mott. Although Mott was a golf-player and that activity was frowned upon at the time, the group decided that he ought to be invited to preach a trial Sunday sermon anyway. When he accepted the invitation and the congregation decided that they liked what they heard, Reverend Nolan Mott was hired in June of 1975 as the third full-time pastor of the Bryant Community Church.

During Reverend Mott's term of service, several new members were added to the church and two additional baptismal services were conducted. More improvements to the building and grounds were made as well, including the addition of a fellowship hall, rest rooms, sanctuary carpeting, walkway canopies, additional paved parking, and vinyl siding for the building.

SIBYL (JONES) CHANCEY

When Reverend Mott retired in 1989, Revered W. W. Whitley became the next pastor. Upon Whitley's resignation not too long thereafter, a committee consisting of members George and Jackie Houghton were appointed to handle a search for his replacement. With the help of other church members, the Houghton's located Reverend Marvin McElhannon to serve as the next pastor. He was hired in November of 1991.

One charter member, Sibyl Chancey, who in her working career was a teacher at Bryant School, deserves special mention for her devoted support of the church over the years it has been in service. Sibyl Alice (Jones) Chancey was a resident of Bryant from 1926 to April 22, 2011, when she passed away at the age of 100 years, 11 months, and 9 days. Her life revolved around her family, her church, and her teaching. She was a loyal member of Bryant Community Church, which she helped construct and where she served in numerous capacities. For as long as she was alive, she was actively involved in just about every activity that was required to sustain the church—community outreach, fund raising, building upkeep, and so on. Because she did as much as anyone could to help the congregation grow and prosper, Sibyl Chancey is remembered with great fondness by those who knew her.

George Houghton (next page) is yet another individual who deserves special mention for his efforts over the years on behalf of the church. Among other things, he became known for willingly tending to the on-going series of plumbing and other problems that had to be dealt with to keep the building comfortable and functional for Sunday school and regular services. He became, in effect, a maintenance specialist for the building, and for his good work in that area as well as others he grew to be much appreciated and is well remembered by members of the church.

Today, the Bryant Community Church remains the same community focal point it has always been. Reverend Robert Honnicutt of Henryetta (next page) is the current pastor, and the congregation has 28 active members. The church has been a source of comfort, inspiration, and support to many during its period of community service, and it continues to do the same today. All the old stores and the schools of Bryant are long gone and there aren't nearly as many people living in the area as there used to be, but the beautiful little Bryant Community Church still stands ready to point old-timers and newcomers alike to the eternal city toward which all its works are dedicated.

*GEORGE
HOUGHTON*

*REVEREND
ROBERT HONNICUTT*

*MIKE MARTIN AND SON DAMEN,
DURING A VISIT TO BRYANT*

BRYANT COMMUNITY
INTERDENOMINATIONAL CHURCH IN 1953

OPAL CHANCEY

VERA (ROSS) CHANCEY

DEDICATION

OF

THE BRYANT COMMUNITY CHURCH

DECEMBER 13, 1953

2 P.M.

PARTICIPATING MINISTERS

FROM THE HENRYETTA MINISTERIAL ALLIANCE

E.W. PETERS, PASTOR FIRST PRESBYTERIAN CHURCH
PRESIDING

M.G. FERGUSON, PASTOR FIRST CHRISTIAN CHURCH
READING OF THE SCRIPTURES

R.G. HARRIS, PASTOR FIRST METHODIST CHURCH
THE SERMON

W.H. DEITZ, PASTOR OF FIRST NAZARENE CHURCH
PRAYER

Dedication of the Bryant Community Interdenominational Church
December 13, 1953 — Page 1

THE ORDER OF SERVICE

PRELUDE

THE ACT OF OPENING THE DOOR OF THE CHURCH

"OPEN TO ME THE GATES OF RIGHTEOUSNESS;
WILL GO INTO THEM, AND I WILL PRAISE THE
PRAISE THE LORD."

HYMN - "THE CHURCH'S ONE FOUNDATION"

PEACE BE TO THIS HOUSE, AND TO ALL WHO
WORSHIP THEREIN.
PEACE BE TO THOSE THAT ENTER, AND TO THOSE
THAT GO OUT THEREFROM.
PEACE BE TO THOSE THAT LOVE IT, AND THAT
LOVE THE NAME OF JESUS CHRIST OUR LORD.
LIFT UP YOUR HEADS, O YE GATES;
EVEN LIFT THEM UP, YE EVERLASTING DOORS;
AND THE KING OF GLORY SHALL COME IN.
WHO IS THIS KING OF GLORY?
THE LORD OF HOSTS,
HE IS THE KING OF GLORY.

THE GLORIA PATRI

THE LESSONS FROM THE HOLY SCRIPTURES:
I KINGS 8:22,23,27-30
I CORINTHIANS 3:10-23
MATTHEW 16:13-20

THE PRAYER OF INVOCATION

STATEMENT BY THE PRESIDING MINISTER

A HYMN OF PRAISE

THE LITANY OF DEDICATION (MINISTER & CONG.)

FOR AS MUCH AS IT PLEASED ALMIGHTY GOD TO PUT
INTO THE HEART OF HIS SERVANTS TO BUILD THIS

Dedication of the Bryant Community Interdenominational Church
December 13, 1953 — Page 2

HOUSE FOR HIS WORSHIP, LET US NOW FULFILL THE GODLY
PURPOSE FOR WHICH WE ARE ASSEMBLED OF DEDICATING IT
TO THE HONOR OF GOD'S MOST HOLY NAME.

GOD AND FATHER OF OUR LORD JESUS CHRIST, OUR FATHER
WHO ART IN HEAVEN:

CONGREGATION: TO THEE WE DEDICATE THIS HOUSE.

LORD JESUS, SON OF GOD, SAVIOUR OF THE WORLD, HEAD
OF THE BODY WHICH IS THE CHURCH:

CONGREGATION: TO THEE WE DEDICATE THIS HOUSE.

SPIRIT OF GOD, GIVEN TO BE OUR ABIDING TEACHER,
SANCTIFIER, AND COMFORTER; LORD AND GIVER OF LIFE:

CONGREGATION: TO THEE WE DEDICATE THIS HOUSE.

PRAYER OF DEDICATION:

O ETERNAL GOD, BE PRESENT WITH US WHO ARE HERE
GATHERED TOGETHER TO DEDICATE THIS HOUSE TO
THY GLORY, SEPARATING IT HENCEFORTH FROM ALL
UNHALLOWED AND COMMON USES. GRANT THAT THIS
HOUSE MAY BE A HABITATION OF THY GLORY, SO THAT
ALL WHO SEEK THY PRESENCE HERE MAY BEHOLD THINE
EVERLASTING LIGHT, AND BE SATISFIED WITH THINE
ETERNAL LOVE, THROUGH JESUS CHRIST OUR LORD.
HERE MAY THE FAITHFUL FIND SALVATION, AND THE
CARELESS BE AWAKENED. HERE MAY THE DOUBTING FIND
FAITH, AND THE ANXIOUS BE ENCOURAGED. HERE MAY
THE TEMPTED FIND HELP, AND THE SORROWFUL COMFORT.
HERE MAY THE WEARY FIND REST, AND THE STRONG BE
RENEWED. HERE MAY THE AGED FIND CONSOLATION, AND
THE YOUNG BE INSPIRED. AMEN.

THE DECLARATION:

IN THE NAME OF THE FATHER, AND OF THE SON, AND
OF THE HOLY GHOST, I NOW DECLARE THIS HOUSE TO BE
FOREVER SET APART FROM ALL PROFANE AND COMMON USES

Dedication of the Bryant Community Interdenominational Church
December 13, 1953 — Page 3

AND CONSECRATED TO THE WORSHIP AND SERVICE OF
ALMIGHTY GOD; TO WHOM BE GLORY AND MAJESTY,
DOMINION AND POWER, FOR EVER AND EVER. AMEN.

PRESENTATION OF THE KEYS TO MR. J.L. JONES

I DELIVER TO YOU THE KEYS OF THIS BUILDING
ERECTED FOR THE BRYANT COMMUNITY CHURCH, AND PRAY
THAT IT MAY BE USED FAITHFULLY FOR THE HIGH
PURPOSES TO WHICH IT HAS BEEN DEDICATED.

A HYMN OF JOY

SERMON BY THE REVEREND R.G. HARRIS

THE OFFERTORY
THE DOXOLOGY

THE BENEDICTION :

THE PEACE OF GOD, WHICH PASSETH ALL UNDERSTANDING,
KEEP YOUR HEARTS AND MINDS IN THE KNOWLEDGE AND
LOVE OF GOD, AND OF HIS SON, JESUS CHRIST, OUR
LORD: AND THE BLESSING OF GOD ALMIGHTY, FATHER,
SON, AND HOLY SPIRIT, BE UPON YOU AND REMAIN WITH
YOU ALWAYS. AMEN.

Dedication of the Bryant Community Interdenominational Church
December 13, 1953 — Page 4

FORMER PASTORS OF THE BRYANT COMMUNITY CHURCH
Among the former pastors were Reverend B. L. Williams (left), shown with his wife, Reverend Nolan Mott (right), shown with his wife Ola, and Reverend Marvin McElhannon (bottom), also shown with his wife.

BRYANT CHRISTIAN NEWS

No. 4	Bryant Community Church	June 1973

A Relevant, Living Theology

We are all aware that many church people feel uneasy talking about Theology. The term either conveys a kind of dogmatic quality - like creedal statements one subscribes to - or else it points to an area of professional activity which has little, if anything, to do with the church and the Christian life as most of us experience it.

The attitude toward theology was not always so. Before seminaries were established in the modern sense, theology centered in the church and came to fullest expression in the life of the church, embodied in sermon and other instructional activities.

In setting "A Relevant, Living Theology" as a basic priority for the people of the Bryant Community, we must acknowledge the importance of a Church in the community and seeing the life of the Church once again as the basic source of theology. You can't improve the techniques of your trade by watching programs on TV, reading a newspaper, or reading advertisements. Neither can you improve your beliefs and the driving forces of your soul without attending and participating in a Church. This helps you to get a fresh view of what theology is all about, one closer to the pulse of a lived Christian and hence "relevant and living". To believe in a "Living Bible" you must have a "Living Theology". We might say then, that theology is the Church's attempt to understand its life in terms faithful to Jesus Christ.

In the first place theology is an on going dialog, because of attempt to understand our life is as continuous as life itself. The participants in the dialog are the people of God, i.e, you and I and all serious Church members, and not just theological experts. Their role is to clarify and enrich the dialog, but not to take it over. To understand theology in this perspective is to open it up to full participation by pastors and lay people alike.

Won't you join us in worship and study so that all our lives may be enriched.

John Underwood, Pastor

****

ITEMS OF INTEREST

Missionary collection for May $20.30

Our attendance for May has been low. Where is the Easter Sunday crowd that made us all so happy? We are looking for all of you back in Church during June. We miss the children and young people.

June 17th is the day to honor the fathers, and may many of them be in attendance.

An Issue of the Bryant Christian News
June, 1963 — Page 1

The church is planning another rummage sale with many things you may always have wanted but never bought. Now you can buy them cheap. Watch the newspaper for time and place.

1973 marks the 20th anniversary of our Bryant Community Church. Many who long years ago moved away said they were so very proud that Bryant finally built a Church. Those now living in the community should be just as proud and help support it with your attendance and talents. Come next Sunday! Plans are in the making for an anniversary dinner in the future.

****

SICKNESS

Home:
       Mrs. Betty Penequine recovering from major surgery.

I want to take this time and space to say it was very thoughtful of you all to send the beautiful cards and remember me in your prayers. A "Special Thanks" to each and every one of you.

                                        Betty Penequine

CHRISTIAN SYMPATHY TO:

The Ayers family in the loss of their sister, Manie.

The Chancey family in the loss of their husband, father and brother, Marvin M. Chancey, who was a charter member of the Bryant Community Church.

****

Behold, I stand at the door and knock: if any man hear my voice, and open the door, I will come in to him and will sup with him and he with me.

****

SERMONS FOR JUNE

3 rd When is Weakness an Asset?

10 th God's Strength in Your Weakness

17 th The Folly of Self-Confidence

24 th The Miracles of God

****

Love God with all your heart.

Do His will in all things.

Then believe things turn out best for all those that love Him and
do His will.

An Issue of the Bryant Christian News
June, 1963 — Page 2

Whether we live a short time or
a long time is unimportant to God.
It is how we live while we are here
and when we die.

Wise sayings often fall on
barren ground, but a kind
word is never thrown away.

BRYANT COMMUNITY CHURCH
Route 1 Box 252
Weleetka, Oklahoma 74880

An Issue of the Bryant Christian News
June, 1963 – Page 3

PASTORS OF BRYANT COMMUNITY CHURCH		
Name	*From*	*To*
Reverend B. L. Williams	*1955*	*1963*
Reverend John Underwood	*1963*	*1974*
Reverend Nolan Mott	*1975*	*1989*
Reverend W. W. Whitley	*1989*	*1991*
Reverend Marvin McElhannon	*1991*	*2004*
Reverend Robert Honnicutt	*2005*	

BRYANT COMMUNITY CHURCH

CHAPTER 10

CAUSES OF BRYANT'S DECLINE

When Oklahoma became the forty-sixth State of the Union on November 16, 1907, Bryant's settlers firmly believed that they were on a road toward continued growth and prosperity at their location in what until only a very few years before had been known as the Oklahoma Indian Territory. They remained excited by their prospects, and, in photographs that were taken during these times, their feelings of confidence and optimism shows clearly on many faces. Sadly, though, for the majority of those who settled in the area, economic life during the 1910's and 1920's was about as good as it ever got. When the 1930's rolled around, residents of Bryant were confronted by a series of economic blows that turned out to be way too much for them to handle.

THE GREAT DEPRESSION

Documentation on file in the Oklahoma State Archives confirms that Oklahoma was especially hard hit by the Great Depression of the 1930's and that within the state the northeastern counties suffered as much and probably more than most of the others. Several factors have been cited to explain the negative difference. First, by 1930 some 62 percent of all the farms in Oklahoma were tenant operated, but in the northeast eight counties that total was exceeded by as much as 18 percent. Second, average farm income in the area was calculated to be only $1018 per year, which was around 35 percent less than the average farm income for the State of Oklahoma as a whole. Third, average farm income had fallen to only 42 percent of what it had been a decade earlier. There was plenty of misery in the farm economy to go around in those days, but the record indicates that economic difficulties were more acute in the northeastern counties than in the rest of the State.

Manufacturing, by the way, according to archived records, didn't fare any better in those days. Wages paid by manufacturers decreased by 20 percent between 1931 and 1933, and, due to the economic importance of Tulsa, this, too, had additional significant negative impact on the northeastern counties of the State. What made matters even worse for the northeastern counties was the fact that, from 1927 forward, bank failures were occurring there with increasing rapidity.

By the time Franklin Roosevelt took office in 1933, about 13 million people, or around 25 percent of the national labor force, were out of work, and many of these people had used up all of their personal savings and had sold all they owned to avoid outright starvation. Roosevelt and his team were opposed to what was referred to at the time as *the dole,* or the giving of cash money to people, but he and his cabinet believed that drastic action had to be taken to head off the possibility of starvation facing many people around our country. In a relatively short period of time, he and his cabinet worked with Congress to pass a long list of social legislation designed to help people cope with effects of the depression, legislation that was packaged and publicized as *The New Deal.*

Under one *alphabet agency* heading or another, projects were implemented in Oklahoma and in every other state to deal effectively with the depression. Congress established the Works Progress Administration, or WPA, on May 6, 1935, to put people to work in *useful local public works projects* as a means of providing immediate employment to those on relief who could not find work elsewhere. Over time, more than 2 million were employed by the WPA in any given month in a variety of public works projects around the country. During its existence, the WPA ended up spending more that $11 billion on 250,000 public projects around the nation. There's little doubt that there was some wasted money and effort associated with the program, but there's also no doubt that the WPA provided a new start for many who might otherwise have gone hungry at the time.

Of the almost $12 billion the WPA received, more than $185 million was expended in Oklahoma. In the State, as elsewhere, the WPA sponsored a number of different programs for the unemployed. Among these were the Federal Art Project, the Federal Writer's Project, the Historical Records Survey, the Federal Music Project, the Federal Theater Project, and adult hospital aide training. Few of these programs, however, were designed to provide employment for unskilled laborers, which was the class of people who made up the largest percentage of the relief rolls in Oklahoma and in its northeastern counties. To help these folks, the WPA organized a massive program of public buildings and facilities construction. Because of the size of the operation, the type of work it performed, and its 75 percent share of the total budget, the WPA public works program benefited more of Oklahoma's unemployed, had a greater impact socially, and left a physical legacy that was—and, in many cases, still is—more apparent than the activities of other social service programs.

The WPA program in Oklahoma was entirely a federal government operation. Organized into one state, eight district and fourteen area offices, it was administered by officials who answered directly to supervisors in Washington, DC. The agency determined the eligibility of people seeking work, selected workers of the type needed, set the wage scale to be paid, and saw to it that Federal Treasury checks were issued for any work that was accomplished. Construction projects undertaken by the WPA were planned and sponsored by local governmental units (cities and counties), which also shared in the costs—an average of 25 percent statewide by 1940. Although there were exceptions, sponsors of these activities generally provided materials while the agency supplied a supervised labor force. National guidelines dictated that particular projects had to be (a) "useful" and (b) limited in cost to $52,000, exclusive of local matching funds or equivalencies.

Between 1935 and 1943, when the agency was abolished, the WPA public works program in Northeastern Oklahoma undertook a large number of state and locally sponsored projects. Most numerous were those involving the construction of roads and streets, bridges, culverts, sidewalks, curbs, sanitation and public health projects (especially malarial control ditches, sanitary privies, water treatment and delivery systems), flood control dams, pasture terraces and gully control work, and airports and runways. More visible, although requiring a smaller percentage of the total labor force, were public buildings, recreational facilities, and cemetery improvements. Aside from sidewalks and culverts, these latter projects are the ones that most people today associate with the work of the WPA.

Before the program ended, the agency's huge employment program in Oklahoma had produced, to cite some specific figures, 2,712 bridges and viaducts, 50,306 culverts, 585 miles of curbs, 68 miles of guttering, 236 miles of malarial control ditches, 94,644 sanitary privies, and a whole list of water and sewage facilities. What's pertinent here is that a fair number of all these projects were completed in Northeastern Oklahoma, and some were completed in Okmulgee County. Today, most WPA-built structures and facilities have out-lived their usefulness, but not all. Some WPA-built buildings, bridges, culverts along country roads, and curbing and guttering are still in use around the State.

Symbolically as well as concretely, the significance of the WPA program in Oklahoma can hardly be overestimated. The public buildings, recreational facilities, and cemetery improvements that were completed in those days indicate the economic importance of the total WPA construction program in Northeastern Oklahoma. At a time when employable people had no jobs and faced the possibility of starvation, the WPA provided meaningful work and at least some financial security. The $31.20 per month that was paid to unskilled workers wasn't much, but for some it was the margin between life and death. Of the 51,292 monthly average number of WPA workers employed in Oklahoma between 1935 and 1941, some 35 percent, or almost 18,000, lived in the northeastern counties. Their collective salaries poured more than one-half million dollars a month into the local economies, an infusion that unquestionably enabled many small retailers in these counties to stay in business when they would otherwise have gone under.

It is also often pointed out that the program produced economic benefits that went beyond wage payments. In its public building program, for example, the WPA utilized unskilled workmen as masons and carpenters. Over time these workers learned crafts that, at a later date, enabled them to enter the employed work force as skilled laborers. The morale of workers was elevated by the knowledge that they had received training that increased their readiness to earn a living.

Had there been no WPA school building or school improvement projects in Okmulgee County during the Thirties, it is likely that many of the school buildings that were in service back then would have been condemned and forced to close. The problem at the time was that most school districts had reached the limit of their bonded indebtedness, which made further issues of debt impossible because assessed valuations of property declined as the depression drug on. Very simply, many school districts needed WPA projects, just to stay afloat. In some school districts, the WPA school building program deserves being thought of as a Godsend to the local educational system. The WPA-funded projects that were completed at Bryant weren't individually large, but they were a great help at the time.

Even with the help supplied by various government programs, however, by 1932 economic hardship all around Oklahoma had become severe. In seven of the nineteen counties in the northeastern quadrant of the state, farm tax delinquencies reached a level of 70 percent and in all counties relief rolls had increased rapidly. By October of 1934, eight counties had 50 percent or more and seven had 20 to 49 percent of their local families on relief. In fact, 31 percent of all the Oklahoma families on relief rolls lived in the nineteen northeastern counties. By any economic measurement, the population of northeastern Oklahoma was caught up in dire circumstances by 1935, and many residents of Bryant suffered just like others around the State.

"DUST BOWL" FARMING CONDITIONS

Overlapping the Great Depression, the Bryant area was also impacted by what came to be referred to as the *Dust Bowl* era of severe drought and wind that created great damage in dry land farming areas across much of the United States during the 1930's. The problem was at its worst in the plains states from the Dakotas to Texas, but other areas, including large swathes of Oklahoma, were adversely affected as well. Dry land farming had always been an iffy proposition, but the high and prolonged winds and drought of the Thirties was really devastating to many of these farmers. When water sources dried up, crops died in the fields and farm animals suffered. Drought conditions had a devastating effect on farmers and, in turn, on the farm laborers and small town merchants and professionals who indirectly depended on farm income for a living. The Dust Bowl was centered in the panhandle areas of Texas and Oklahoma and in parts of Kansas, Colorado, and New Mexico, but, again, peripheral areas, areas such as Bryant, suffered as well.

PROGRESS IN AGRICULTURAL MECHANIZATION

The economic viability of small farm towns like Bryant was also undermined by industrialization that was taking place throughout our country, specifically in the form of large-scale mechanized farming operations. Census figures for the 1920's show that although the population of the United States had grown to 106 million people, for the first time in our national history more people were living in city areas than on farms in the country. Most still lived in very small cities at the time, but it was clear that a significant shift in the kinds of work people were doing had taken place. More and more people had begun to work in stores, factories, and service businesses than on farms—large or small. The movement of people from small farm towns to larger cities really hurt places like Bryant.

Even harder hit than small town farmers and merchants were tenant farmers and sharecroppers, people who barely made a living even in the best of times. The desire to own their own land was the primary force that drew people to the town in the first place, but over the years only a relative few families were able to build up successful agricultural operations. What turned out to be far more common was that families had to struggle to eke an existence out of the small dry land farms and ranches that existed in the area. Again, making a living at Bryant was never easy.

Tenant farmers operated on leased or rented land, but they were often not much better off than sharecroppers. Many of them stayed deeply in debt to local landowners and merchants and barely made a living. Given the laws and customs of the times, tenant and sharecropper families were effectively prevented from leaving their rented homesteads if they owed money to anyone. Many were never able to dig their way out of debts that tended to increase with each passing year, and they became trapped in the system. For some the cycle was broken only when they were effectively forced off the land after farm prices collapsed during the depression years.

CLOSURES OF MINING AND PETROLEUM OPERATIONS

During the 1930's, the mining sector of Oklahoma's economy fared just as badly as agriculture. When many of the lead, zinc, and coal mines that had brought such great prosperity to the Bryant area began to close down, even more thousands of people were forced to move away in search of work.

A similar problem occurred in the petroleum industry. Between 1929 and 1934, oil production, most of which took place in the northeastern counties, decreased by as much as 30 percent. This turn of events put even more people out of work, and they, too, were forced to move elsewhere in search of employment.

SCHOOL CONSOLIDATIONS

There's no doubt that the decline of Bryant was hastened when the high school had to be closed down at the end of the 1956-57 academic year due to lack of enrollment. When enrollment continued to decline during the 1950's, the elementary school eventually had to be closed down as well. In the absence of convenient access to schooling for their children, more families were forced to move out of the area and new families could not be drawn in to replace them.

THE END OF THE LINE

It was through a slow and excruciatingly painful process that lasted over many years that Bryant gradually declined to the scattering of rural homes and farms that are to be found there today. The combined adverse effects of the Great Depression, Dust Bowl drought conditions, agricultural mechanization, layoffs in the mining and petroleum industries, and the closure of all the local schools were way too much for the town to overcome. Without enough industry or farming activity to provide dependable employment, even those who would have preferred to stay in the area could not afford to do so. Very simply, lack of economic opportunity forced people to move away in search of new ways of making a living. Bryant, in other words, simply faded away as an economically viable town site.

Bryant met a fate not unlike that of many of other small farm towns that used to exist throughout Oklahoma and the rest of the so-called Dust Bowl states, towns that never became as prosperous as their early settlers hoped and thought they would. Instead, just the opposite occurred, and many of them died out— again, not for a single reason, but for many. It is only natural for us to wonder today how and why things got so far off track back then, since, from our comfortable vantage point, it's hard to understand how such an outcome could have come to pass. Even though very few homes or other landmarks remain visible from the old days of Bryant, just looking at the few landmarks that do remain is more than enough to bring a lump to the throats of those who recall what the town and school used to be like. That's how it is for me, anyway, and I think there are others out there who feel exactly the same way!

THE SCHOOLS OF BRYANT IN 1988

After Bryant High School was shut down at the end of the 1957 school year and Bryant Elementary School was closed in the 1960s, the two old brick buildings as well as the gymnasium that was attached to the back of the high school gradually began to deteriorate. People lived (or squatted?) in the grade school for a while, but the deterioration continued until the structures became a hazard. At that point, Homer Chancey bought the buildings and had them torn down. Today, the site where they once stood is so overgrown by brush and shrubbery that it is all but impossible to tell that they were ever there at all. The buildings came to a sad end, at least from the standpoint of those who have fond memories of having taught or attended school there at one time.

Close-up view of the grammar school before it was razed.

An interior view of one of the classrooms of Bryant Elementary School, showing how the building had been trashed by squatters before it finally fell into ruins.

*Joe
Asbury*

ASBURY FAMILY MEMBERS IN 1954

*Descendents of Creek Indian Joshua Asbury, donor of the
allotment land that became the site of the Town of Bryant*

Carol Asbury

Wesley Asbury

*MIKE MARTIN WITH HIS SON DAMEN,
VIEWING THE FARM POND BEHIND HIS CHILDHOOD
HOME SITE DURING A VISIT TO BRYANT*

CHAPTER 11

THE *"OKIE MIGRATION"*

In the mid-1930's, prospects for getting ahead in the world must have seemed hopelessly bleak to people all around the country, but this perception had to have been even more deeply felt among those who lived in isolated country towns such as Bryant. Economic opportunity was so lacking in rural areas of its kind that a good number of people had to go to bed hungry during this period of time. It came as no surprise to anyone, therefore, when residents of these small rural towns began leaving their homes in search of stable employment. Because so many of the people who went *out on the road* in those days were from Oklahoma, it wasn't long before "Okies" became a common collective term for all *Dustbowlers*, regardless of what state they were actually from.

California became a destination for a good number of folks from Bryant as well as from other small towns in Oklahoma simply because word got around that there was work to be found there during those hard economic times. It was common for those who sought work out there to depart on exploratory trips at first, trips that were intended to be temporary rather than permanent. Later on, however, as people became more familiar with what there was out west, many began staying away for longer and longer periods of time, until, finally, some stopped coming back at all.

By the time the period of economic hardship receded, in some cases entire extended families had moved away from small towns in rural Oklahoma for a fresh start in California or some other western state. In fact, so many people moved out of the economically depressed and drought-ridden central states in those days that demographers and researchers eventually began to describe their overall movement as an *internal migration*, a significant shift in where people lived within our country. Individual families simply *moved*, but because so many of them did it at roughly the same time their collective activities really did amount to a mass movement—in fact, a great internal migration.

During this period of time, many poorer families left their homes carrying only as much of their belongings as they could pack onto a single car or truck for the trip out west, which was often made to an only generally known destination. Others hitchhiked, jumped on railroad boxcars, or teamed up with friends to get there. Many had very little in the way of money, and more than a few were nearly destitute.

For families with little in the way of resources, it was common practice to camp along the highway as they traveled west, pulling off the road wherever the basic requirements of a campsite happened to be spotted—a safe place to park, a source of water, wood or brush for a fire, and space to throw out blankets for the night. They gathered firewood from wherever it could be found, and many a mother got used to cooking over campfires and caring for children on roadsides or riverbanks, not only during the trip out west but also, in a good number of cases, for a period of time after their arrival in California.

Car troubles such as flat tires, overheated radiators, dead batteries, and other mechanical problems were common along the way, given the often already rundown cars and trucks in which many of these families traveled. Because they had little money to live on and even less, therefore, to spend on repairs, it wasn't uncommon to travel in fear of more serious breakdowns—engine or transmission problems, for example. For a good many *Okie* travelers, the trip out west was anything but a carefree journey.

Members of the paternal (Martin) and maternal (Edwards) sides of my own family were typical of the many Oklahomans who began making trips to California during the late 1930's, through the 1940's, and even on up to the early 1950's. Spurred by a pressing need to find work, they made trip after trip to the central San Joaquin Valley in search of seasonal employment or, better still, any regular jobs they could find. It was their practice to do what they could to treat these journeys as larks or adventures, but all of them knew very well that they were just doing what needed to be done.

During my childhood, members of the paternal side of my family, the Martins, spoke from time to time of one particular trip among many they made out west, since it was one they knew in advance would be different from all their others. In the first place, it was known that, if the trip went well, several of them intended to stay in California permanently. Secondly, they knew they were going to make the trip in a nearly new 1939 Chevy half-ton pickup truck, which meant that they'd be traveling in a more mechanically sound and comfortable vehicle than in the past.

The nearly new truck was owned by George Jackson Martin, my paternal grandfather, who bought it for $600 on a time payment plan he worked out with Loan Officer Peyster of the Morris State Bank using down payment money scraped together through selling hogs, hauling cotton seed, doing odd jobs, and getting rid of just about every other asset he had at the time. As the senior member of the group that would be making the trip, he was bound and determined, he declared before leaving to anyone who would listen, that they weren't going to have to worry about any breakdowns along the road this time around.

Actually, at least some of the money pulled together to finance Grandpa's new truck was provided by his sons, inasmuch as it was a rule in his household for wages any of them earned while they lived under his roof would automatically be turned over to him. Until his sons were married and living in households of their own, it was their father who decided if and when they were to have any spending money. In those days it still made economic sense for a man to have a lot of sons, and it wasn't at all uncommon for household income to be handled in this way. The only social security system most rural people had to rely on back then, it must be remembered, was a large family.

Well before the travelers left town, everyone in the community knew that the Martin's were planning a trip out west in their nearly new truck, since everybody knew everybody in town in those days, usually on a first name basis; most had known one another, in fact, for their entire lives. Because it made a lot of sense to share expenses during tough economic times, several neighbors had either been invited or had asked to go along on the trip. By the time the day of departure rolled around, fourteen people had signed up to go along—George and Virginia Martin, their son William David "Dub" and his wife Lola (Tinny) Martin, their unmarried sons Charlie, Robert, Dempsey, and George "Sonny" Martin, their daughter Naomi Martin, Joyce Bean, Mary Lou and Jimmy Hart and their two children, plus Dub Martin's dog. Even though several of the travelers were children, these numbers must have made for a very cozy journey!

As they pulled out of town on a July morning in the early Forties and headed out in the direction of California, everyone felt excited and happy (and probably, I would imagine, more that a little bit tentative and nervous) to finally be out on the road. George Martin's eldest son Dub did most of the driving, with his mother and father riding beside him in the front seat. The others rode in the bed of the truck, sitting on jerry-rigged benches or on floor padding made of blankets. A temporary canvas top had been rigged to enclose the truck bed as a shelter, giving the rig a tent-like look. (On other occasions, they used a solid enclosure that was equipped with a ladder to get to the top, making it look like a big box.)

Members of the group recalled sleeping one night during this trip out west in a cabin aside a bubbling stream somewhere around St. John's, Arizona. Most of their stops, however, were spent camped beside the highway, where some slept in the truck while other slept on blankets spread on the ground. They ate meals of beans and potatoes in the evenings and pancakes in the mornings, all prepared over campfires using water drawn from rivers or from service stations faucets.

Due to stopovers caused mainly by financial problems, the trip to California ended up taking over a month. They were delayed first by making several wrong turns along the way, and they were delayed again near Flagstaff, Arizona, by a creek flood. When they nearly ran out of food before the water went down, Mary Lou bought a five pound block of cheese and a large box of crackers that everyone shared until all of it was eaten. When their money ran low due to the delays, they hired on to work for several weeks at a logging camp near Flagstaff owned by a man by the name of "Snow" Anthony. Snow was an ex-Okmulgee County resident who operated a small sawmill on government-owned land under terms of a contract that permitted him to cut out diseased and fallen timber for forest protection. They worked for Snow until they earned enough money to get back out on the road again. During their stay in Arizona, some of the travelers recalled killing a large rattlesnake and watching forest station rangers break horses in a corral that was located near where they were camped. As it turned out, they recalled, a few members of the group liked Arizona so much they decided to stay there rather than go on to California.

The rest of the group, however, eventually made it to Riverbank, California, a small town located on the south side of the Stanislaus River near the center of the San Joaquin Valley, where they found work at one of the many peach orchards that were there at the time, just as they are today. Early during their stay, they picked peaches at a pay rate of *5¢ per 48 pound box for the good ones and 3¢ per box for the bad ones*. Later on, some landed jobs at the Darpenian Dry Yard, where their rate of pay jumped to 15¢ per hour. After signing up for *Social Security Cards* in order to take advantage of one of the Roosevelt administration's new anti-depression programs, everyone thought they really were well on the way toward achieving at least some higher degree of financial security. When work ran out around Riverbank, they moved on to other San Joaquin Valley towns in search of other field or orchard jobs.

At the time, many native Californians looked upon even the most hard-working and law-abiding of the "Okies" as being up to no good and, therefore, did what they could to make sure they knew they were unwelcome. Members of the Martin family got personally acquainted with this attitude one day in the early Forties on the outskirts of Porterville when George, Dub, Walker, Charlie, Robert, and Dempsey Martin pulled off a farm to market road and up a dirt drive toward a farm house next to an orchard of ripe fruit intent upon asking the grower, a man by the name of Cantrell, for work. Upon noting their nearly new truck and the fact that the men in it were cleanly and nicely dressed, the grower immediately jumped to the conclusion that he was being confronted by agitators or organizers of one kind or another. Without a word of warning, he stepped out on the porch of his home and shot at the truck with a high-powered deer rifle in an effort to run them off!

Even before the job seekers had a chance to step out and say what they were there for, the round he fired smashed through the front windshield of the truck, creating a bloody wound on Dub's face caused by flying shards of glass. After tearing away from the home and orchard as fast as they could in an absolute panic, the irate men rushed Dub to town for treatment by a local doctor. Once his wounds were cared for, they returned to the farm accompanied by police officers, intent upon having the grower arrested for assault. Cantrell eventually had to appear in court, but, even though he had almost killed three men without any real warning or justification, in the end he received no jail time at all. The incident was caused by a case of mistaken identity, it was determined, and Cantrell had only been trying to protect his property. It was well know by locals that he had been having trouble with *organizers and rabble rousers* out at his place. The incident was reported in an article in the local newspaper, the Porterville Recorder.

It was just accepted back then that "Okies" who got down on their luck in the environment that prevailed usually had to rough things out on their own. Early on, little or no social service assistance was available to them in California, which meant that people who were having trouble just had to pitch camp and wait out their hardships, living off the land and surviving on menial work and near-starvation wages. Many barely got by. When their money and food ran out, some became so desperate that they pilfered and stole, just to survive. Ignored as they were by local relief agencies, many had nowhere else to turn. Even as they struggled to keep body and soul together, newspapers and commentators routinely put down and criticized them while they were down and out, describing them as "*Okies*" or "*Dust Bowl Refugees*" or "*Arkies*" and openly suggesting that *they ought to go back where they came from!*

After the fact, researchers have pointed out that it was out of fear more than anything else that Californians lashed out at "Okies" at the time. The truth is that they feared them, say the researchers, not just due to the potential of danger to their person or property, but due to the fact that the very existence of so many poor and desperate people in their back yards caused them to worry about their own well being. The struggles of the Okies, in other words, made them think of what until that time had been the unthought-of possibility that their own economic security might not be quite as certain as they liked to believe. The presence of so many bedraggled people living around them meant that their own worst fears about the scary possibilities of the Great Depression were staring them right in the face; if the Okies could be caught up in such awful poverty, in other words, it could happen to them as well!

What members of poor families had to learn in those days was that when they left their farm communities and their former roles as farmers in their home states, they effectively changed their status in life. Out in California they weren't looked upon as ex-farmers or even ex-farm laborers; they were looked upon as nothing more that *migrant workers*. For the remainder of their lives, some Okie migrants suffered from the consequences of this change in their social status. Some, in fact, were never able to break out of a negative mindset formed by the stress and disorientation they experienced during this period of time. It isn't an easy thing for people to leave behind the kind of life they are used to living. Becoming migrant workers meant that people who had once been concerned only with farm work and hunting and fishing and living a simple life now had to deal with the harsh realities of making new places for themselves in areas where they really weren't welcome. It doesn't take very much study of the record to learn that some of what migrants had to deal with after they arrived in California was miserably harsh and difficult.

Members of my family worked hard and played hard while they were out in California to work in fields and orchards, but for years they always returned to Oklahoma. Even though they went back home, however, with every trip they grew more and more accustomed to living out west. Many younger couples within my extended family made the trip out there again and again over the years, and then, as it turned out, most of them left and just never returned. This same pattern was repeated by thousands of other families of Oklahomans, including many of the families of Bryant. So many left, in fact, that some small farm towns ended up looking almost totally depopulated.

The way this came to pass is that just as soon as one couple within an extended family got settled in California, their relatives began making periodic trips out to visit them, sometimes just to keep in touch and at other times to do seasonal work. The Martin brothers, for example, were especially close in those days, and even those who intended to stay in Oklahoma nevertheless looked forward to their visits with family members and friends who had moved out west. My father, Robert Jackson "Bob" Martin, fell into exactly this category.

Charlie Martin, my Dad's older brother, was the first of George Martin's sons to move to California to stay. After marrying Eva "Evie" Edwards, a daughter of Charlie and Vada (Winkempleck) Edwards of Okmulgee County, he got by when he first got there by doing the same kind of field and orchard piece work members of the family had done in the past. Eventually, though, after moving to the San Joaquin Valley Town of Oakdale, he put down permanent roots. Not too long thereafter, he was able to open a business of his own—a combination service station, garage, restaurant, and bar. After that, with the help of various members of his extended family, he hand-built a home on a lot he purchased on the outskirts of town. Once he and Evie got settled in a home of their own, they went on to have three sons—Charles, David, and Bruce. David died while he was young, but the other two boys grew up and became even more successful in California than their father, who, by the way, also did very well for himself, at least for a while.

Upon noting and being duly impressed by Charlie's success out in California, his older brother Dub moved to Oakdale as well. Not too long thereafter, their father and mother, George and Virginia Martin, my paternal grandparents and their younger children, moved out there too, leaving their third son, Robert, in Oklahoma by himself. Eventually, Robert married Mary Edwards, another daughter of Charlie and Vada Edwards, and therefore a sister of his brother Charlie's wife, Evie. Brothers, in other words, married sisters, which wasn't at all uncommon in those days, at least not among people who grew up in small farm towns.

Robert and Mary started a family of their own in Okmulgee County at that point, and, seemingly quicker than a cat can wink it's eye, they had seven children to care for—Mickey (me), Dickey, Bobby, Tony, Sandy, Tommy, and Ronny. Two more children, Susy and Judy, came along later on. Large families weren't at all uncommon at the time, especially not in rural farming communities.

As a married man, Dad first attempted to earn a living by pursuing his dream of operating a farm of his own. After renting a 40-acre plot of land in northeastern Okmulgee County that others before him had already failed to operate successfully, he began to raise cotton, corn, and potatoes. He intended to buy the farm later on, if things went well. Sadly, though, farming his rental land didn't go any better for him than it had for those who owned it before him. Dry land farming in Oklahoma, he discovered, was every bit the *iffy proposition* friends and family had warned him it was going to be.

Upon his failure in farming, Dad moved our family to a home located on the outskirts of Bryant in southwestern Okmulgee County, a place he rented for $15 per month from an owner who practically begged him to buy it instead, just so he could get it off his hands. *"You can't buy property or anything else when you're flat broke and already in debt,"* Dad recalled telling him, *"even somethin' that can be had for a rock bottom price."*

Even though Dad was able to land a full-time county job driving a road grader, it didn't pay enough for him to be able to dig out of the financial hole he'd gotten himself into after failing as a farmer. With a large and growing family to feed and lots of debt to pay off, it wasn't very long before Dad, like his brothers and parents before him, was itching to try something new. He faced the same reality so many others just like him had bumped up against in the past: A scarcity of good jobs and, even when a job could be found, a prevailing wage rate that was too low to get ahead on.

The way things had worked out, in other words, was that my parents, Robert and Mary Martin, had become the lone and unsuccessful holdouts within a large extended family when it came to staying put in their home at Bryant in rural Okmulgee County. Even though he had taken our family to California again and again to do temporary work in the fields or for visits with his parents and brothers, he had no interest at all in moving out there for good. He loved Oklahoma and Okmulgee County, and that's where he wanted stay.

Even so, after every visit with his successful older brother Charlie and his other siblings and mom and dad out west, he returned home impressed by how much better things seemed to be going for all of them than they were for him. He was especially taken by his older brother Charlie's success in business and the general sense of optimism he projected. His visits out west, in other words, had a tremendous impact on how he looked at life back home. It wasn't long before he began to think that if his brothers had been able to do well in California, then he ought to be able to do the same thing himself. When it came to his desire to stay put in Okmulgee County, his years of unsuccessfully struggling to get ahead finally began to wear down his resolve.

Dad hung on for years before taking seriously the possibility of leaving the area he was born in and the state he loved for an uncertain future out in California. He knew very well that after attending school only sporadically up to the eighth grade, he had very limited skills that could be sold in the job market. About the only non-agricultural work he had done up to that time was to help his Uncle Alvis, who had a side job as a trapper in the town they grew up in, skinning animals for their hides. His Uncle Alvis sold the hides, while dad sold the freshly skinned carcasses for cash by carrying them from door-to-door around town. Fresh meat was highly valued in those days, since many people didn't have ice boxes, much less refrigerators. The game he sold was very popular, especially among black residents of their town.

Nobody needed to tell him that animal skinning and cotton picking were unlikely to be high-paying occupations out in California, thus it was only after years of hesitation that Dad finally decided to follow his older and more daring brother Charlie out west. One summer evening when got home after a hot day of work driving a county road grader, he surprised me, his oldest son, eight years old at the time, by asking in feigned seriousness, "*What do you think, Mick; should we pack up and move to California?*" After a moment of hesitation in which I recalled all the happy vacations we had enjoyed with my cousins, Charles and Bruce, at the home of my prosperous Uncle Charlie, I recall answering in all earnestness, "*Yeah, Dad; I think we should!*" He'd already made up his mind to leave, of course; he just didn't want me, the oldest of his kids, to become upset upon realizing that moving would mean that I'd have to leave behind all the classmates I played with every day at Bryant School.

Only a few days after that brief conversation, my parents decided to "*migrate*" to California. With this decision, every member of my paternal grandparents' (George and Virginia Martin) family had moved out west. Our move, which took place during the 1952-53 school year, was effected by loading as much of what we owned as could fit in our Chevy sedan along with Mom and Dad and the first seven of their nine children and driving away from Oklahoma out toward the *Sunshine State*. Almost everything my parents owned at the time—furniture, guns, and so on—was just abandoned, left sitting right where it was.

Chauvinism was clearly alive and thriving in those days, as indicated by the following comments often repeated by my mother in the wake of Dad's decision to move our family to California: "*I want you to know he sold everything we owned for $350 and then come home and told me about it afterwards and said we was moving to California! I got so mad at him! He never asked me or nothin'; he just done it and then told me it was done. We had to drive off and leave behind everything we had. All we took is what we could load in our car with the two of us and all you kids. Made me so mad I could of wrung his neck!*" My mother's pet name for dad in those days, by the way, was "*Daddy,*" just as it was for all us kids.

Once we got to California the first place we landed was at Hood's Camp on the outskirts of Porterville, the same small cluster of 10' X 18' farm labor cabins located behind a combination grocery store, service station, garage, and used car lot that members of the family had stayed at in the past. It was operated by a couple by the name of Hobert and Ortha Hood. Everyone in my family loved the place, primarily because it was located just across the road from the cotton fields at which we found work and the fact that it had a communal shower and restroom facility out back, one that featured the first residential flush toilet and shower any of us had access to up to that time.

Mom and Dad and all of us kids left the camp each day to do farm labor piecework in the form of picking or hoeing cotton, cutting lemons, picking or swamping peaches, or cleaning fields of pie melons. As our family struggled through years of barely making a living as farm laborers, it is easy to imagine how Dad and Mom must have longed for the good old days of their younger years in the small farm towns they grew up in. Just about anyone, I'm sure, would have had the same kinds of thoughts.

Eventually, though, Dad landed a permanent job and was able to buy a home for our family in the central San Joaquin Valley town of Stockton, where he and mom finally settled down and stayed put. They lived there for the rest of their lives. Earning a living was never easy for them, but in later years they were proud of being able to get all us kids through high school and to see us get married and head out on our own. In addition, Dad was able to build up enough of a retirement for him and mom to be able to travel back to Oklahoma every year to fish and hunt and visit with friends in Oklahoma they had known for their entire lives. He never forgot his early days and the friends of his youth, and there was never any place in the country where he enjoyed vacationing more than at the lakes and river bottoms around his boyhood home town in Okmulgee County, Oklahoma.

With many different variations, a chain of events of the kind that took place within in my own immediate family was repeated within family after family from the poverty-stricken areas of states such as Oklahoma during the years that followed the Great Depression, the Dust Bowl, and the period of agricultural mechanization that so adversely impacted farm economies during those lean times. Some students of the subject have estimated that as many as a million ex-farm workers from that region of the country ultimately wound up living in California, where—at least during the early period of their lives there—their economic situation was in many cases actually worsened rather than improved. It was an episode that didn't end quite as neatly as histories of the period sometimes imply.

Fortunately, though, most of the "migrant" Oklahomans—just like Charlie and Evie and Robert and Mary Martin—did indeed go on to build better lives for themselves and their children in California, just as they had hoped. Today, their children and their children's children are among the teachers, engineers, police officers, and business men and women that make up a significant portion of the working population of the State. In the same way that their fathers and grandfathers before them moved from more eastern states in search of economic opportunity on the Oklahoma Indian Territory frontier, they moved to the agricultural fields of California in search of economic betterment. It's great to be able to say that for each generation in its turn, despite their many problems, the American Dream eventually became a reality. It is very much an open question, as far as I'm concerned, whether or not young couples starting out today will be able to do the same thing. Given the many problems of our own times, happiness and prosperity isn't an outcome that can be taken for granted!

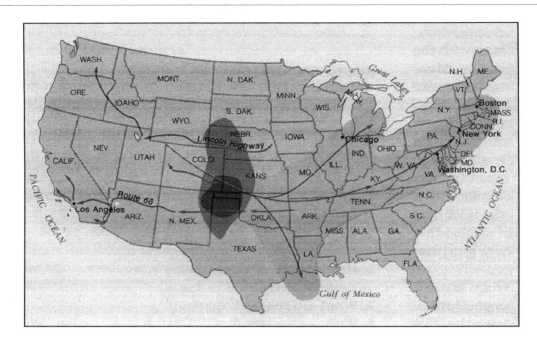

MAP OF THE DUST BOWL OF THE 1930'S

The darkened areas indicate the heart of the drought and wind impacted areas; the arrows indicate prevailing wind direction (eastward) and routes of migration (westward).

SOURCE: Land of Promise: A History of the United States from 1865, Volume 2, by Carol Berkin and Leonard Wood, Copyright© 1986. Pearson Education for Its Affiliates. Used by permission. All Rights Reserved.

DRY LAND FARMER WILLIAM DAVID "DUB" MARTIN, OKMULGEE COUNTY, OKLAHOMA

Lola (Tinny) Martin, wife of William David "Dub" Martin, and nephew Chuck at her family home in Okmulgee County. Dub Martin raised laying hens that produced eggs he could trade for cash or groceries at country stores. At the time, trading for groceries and other essentials was a common practice.

Edwards family and friends who traveled with them on a trip to California, camped for a night beside old Route 66 near Winslow, Arizona, in April, 1943. Flat tires and other mechanical problems were common at the time.

MIDWEST MIGRATION FIFTH OF GREAT FARM LABOR INFLUXES INTO CALIFORNIA, SURVEY SAYS

SACRAMENTO, July 12. (UP)—The influx of Midwest migrants to California during the recent years, represents the fifth great migration in the state's history, according to a report by George Gleason, executive secretary of the Los Angeles county committee for church and community cooperation.

The new migration, however, is the first of native, white Americans. The previous immigrants were Chinese, Japanese, Mexican and Filipino, respectively.

The Chinese, in large numbers, were brought in following the gold rush of 1849, Gleason recounted. They built the railroads and provided the cheap labor for mines and farm. Their immigration was cut off by law in 1888.

Then followed three successive waves of cheap foreign labor. First, the Japanese, whose immigration was checked in 1907 and finally stopped in 1924. Japanese were followed by the Mexicans and by 1920 there were 70,000 Japanese and 80,000 foreign-born Mexicans in California. Filipinos to the number of 31,000 were brought in between 1920 and 1929.

"Since 1934, however," Gleason said, "due to the repatriation of many Mexicans and the cutting off of Filipino immigration, the complexion of the agricultural migrants has literally changed, so that 80 to 90 per cent are now native white Americans."

He pointed out that the migrants are divided into two classes—the habitual migrants, who from choice or habit have been following the harvests, and the removal migrants, who have been forced by low prices, drought and mechanization to seek a better life in another state.

"The latter are truly the dispossessed," Gleason declared. "They form the large part of the 250,000 to 300,000 people who desperately need help in California."

"Orientals and Mexicans, accustomed at home to a lower standard of living, usually bettered their condition event in the rough, unsanitary camp life of the intermittent farm work," he continued, "But now, with the presence in the state of a quarter of a million migrant people whose culture is similar to our own, this fifth migration is presenting a problem which must be promptly faced and wisely solved."

SOURCE: *Porterville Recorder, July 13, 1940.*

FEDERAL CAMPS IN HOME STATES OF MIGRANT FAMILIES PROPOSED BY CALIFORNIA CONGRESSMEN

WASHINGTON, Mar. 12. (U.P.) California congressmen who are opposed to construction of federal migrant camps have proposed creation of reclamation and housing projects in Arkansas and Oklahoma as a solution to the migratory labor problem. Rep. Alfred J. Elliott, D., Calif., who said he spoke for "about 50 per cent" of the California congressional delegation, said that California's problem could not be solved by migrant camp construction "because it makes California too attractive." He proposed creation of projects in their home states, which would induce the migrants to leave California and influence others not to come.

Elliott said he favored a resolution sponsored by Rep. John H. Tolan, D. Calif., to investigate "interstate migration of destitute citizens," but admitted that he thought there was little chance of successfully opposing construction of camps planned for Porterville and Farmersville, Calif.

He voiced his opposition to the camps at a meeting of the California congressional delegation last week, called to discuss the migratory labor problem. This week he plans to introduce a bill to divert some of the funds for camp construction to the support of school districts in which the camps will be located.

Draws More Migrants

"It does no good to build migrant camps," he said, "because that merely draws in more out-of-state workers. They come because California pays higher wages and higher relief and has better social benefits than other states. They know they will be taken care of. While communities from Oklahoma, Arkansas and other states pick up and leave, because their brothers, or uncles or friends write them that they get taken care of in California. There are thousands upon thousands of them, and you couldn't build enough migrant camps to take care of them all.

"But if their land wasn't depleted so they couldn't make a living and if they had decent places to live at home, most of them wouldn't leave. That is the thing to get at. Once a program of reclamation and housing, providing many jobs, was started, and it became known among the migrants, lots of them would leave California to go home."

For these migrants "who won't leave" Elliott favors a federal homestead plan, under which the workers could be given land to pay for over a long period. He said he favored more equal state old age and other benefits, also, to take the burden off California.

"But something has got to be done," he declared. "Not only are these people taking jobs from Californians and crowding their children out of schools, but they are bankrupting counties and school districts. They come in poor health, and are a health menace and at the same time a tremendous health cost. The situation is getting more serious daily. And still more of them come, and they will continue to come, as long as they keep putting migrants up."

SOURCE
Porterville Recorder,
March 12, 1940

SAYS MIGRANTS THREATENING WAGE STANDARD

BAKERSFIELD, Mar. 6.—Migrant settlers are threatening the jobs of California workers, President Arthur S. Crites of the California Citizens' Association warned in an address today.

He pointed out that at the present time there aren't enough jobs in the state to go around and urged that California employers hire residents only. He also urged that California citizens discourage friends and relatives from coming here in hope of finding work.

"There is every indication," Crites said, "notwithstanding our new three-year resident requirement for relief clients, that migration will be heavier than ever in the future due to the depressed condition of agriculture generally.

"The situation of migrants settling in California has become so acute that now our dealings with the problem necessarily spring from motives of self-preservation," Crites added. "Regardless of your line of business, whether you are a laboring man or on a public works project, this situation is going to affect you sooner or later, if it has not hit you already."

In addition to threatening jobs and the probability that wages and living standards will be forced down by competition from migrant labor, Crites pointed out the political dangers.

"With a million more migrants flooding our state, any law might be passed which would strike at the vitals of our economic system and bring wholesale misery to the entire population."

"The last vote upon the Ham and Eggs proposition is indicative of the dangers we face through continued increasing migration. One million more penniless settlers might turn the scales in the opposite direction."

He added that there are six men for every available job in California now, and that every migrant who settles in California is either going to take one of those jobs from a resident of the state or eventually be on the taxpayers' backs as a dole recipient.

SOURCE
Porterville Recorder,
March 6, 1940

William

GEORGE AND VIRGINIA MARTIN

George, Jr.

Charlie

Robert

Dempsey

Naomi

Charlie and Robert Martin in adulthood, during World War II

Hood's Camp, a farm labor camp near Porterville, was one place the Martin family lived after they reached California

A Martin family gathering at Hood's Camp

Charlie Martin and his wife Evie at The Orange Blossom Station, a combination service station, garage, restaurant and bar business he owned on the outskirts of Oakdale, California, hosting a visit by his younger brother Robert and his wife Mary of Bryant, Oklahoma, during the early 1950s.

MARTIN'S ◆NORWALK◆ SERVICE
926 WEST F STREET   -   PHONE 847-9956
TIRES - TUBES - BATTERIES - ACCESSORIES
· OAKDALE, CALIFORNIA ·

DATE _____ 196__

M _____

	GALS. GASOLINE	
	QTS. OIL	
	GREASE	
	WASH	
	POLISH	
	STORAGE	
	VULCANIZING	
	TIRES & TUBES	
	MOTOR CLEANED	
	LABOR	

24

Form 5 – National Press, Inc., North Chicago, Ill.

Robert and Mary Edwards of Okmulgee County, Oklahoma, courted and were married while their families lived at Hood's Camp in Porterville, California. They moved back to Okmulgee County after their marriage, hoping to make a living off a 40-acre farm that looked very much like the one pictured below.

Sisters Eva "Evie" (left) and Mary Edwards, who married brothers Charlie and Robert "Bob" Martin of Okmulgee County

Butchering a hog on Robert Martin's Okmulgee County farm

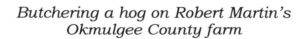

The rhythms of small town life and hunting and fishing for recreation in rural Okmulgee County differed greatly from how the Martin family lived in California.

*Squirrel hunters George and Robert Martin
of Okmulgee County, Oklahoma*

Skinning game at the end of a hunt

Looking south down Maine, the street in front of Bryant School, just before Robert Martin moved his family to California. At the time, this was pretty much all that was left of the Town of Bryant.

The turn off the road between the Towns of Bryant and Henryetta that led to the Martin home at Bryant

*Another view of the turn off the road between the Towns of
Bryant and Henryetta that led to the Martin home at Bryant*

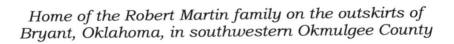

*Home of the Robert Martin family on the outskirts of
Bryant, Oklahoma, in southwestern Okmulgee County*

Okmulgee County Roads District #3 Garage and the road grader driven by Robert Martin.

Robert "Bob" Martin, at around the time he left Bryant.

*Farm pond fishermen
Dickey (left) and Mickey Martin of Bryant*

Bryant Elementary School classmates during the 1952-53 school year. Pictured are Ruby Waters, Wayne Satawake, Millie Haynes, Ronnie White, Jackie Satawake, Dickey Martin, Josephine Satawake, and Mickey Martin.

Mary Martin and children, on one of many trips to California

*Francis Blunt in front of a
cabin at Hood's Camp*

*Mary Martin in front of a
cabin at Hood's Camp*

*Grandmother Virginia Martin posing grandchildren
Dickey, Tony, Mickey, Bobby, and Bruce for
a family photograph at Hood's Camp.*

*DICK MARTIN AND LOLA MARTIN, PICKING
PEACHES IN THE SAN JOAQUIN VALLEY*

*ROBERT AND MARY MARTIN,
DURING THEIR EARLY YEARS IN CALIFORNIA*

*Mary Martin with seven of her nine children
in Oakdale, California*

*Robert and Mary Martin and their children,
at the family home in Stockton, California*

PATERNAL LINEAGE
OF SINGER-COMPOSER DAMEN JACKSON MARTIN,
WHOSE SONG "WEST OF TUCUMCARI" IS PLAYED TO
COMMEMORATE THE MIGRANT JOURNEY
OF THE ELDERS OF HIS FAMILY

Great-Grandfather George Jackson Martin and wife Virginia (top left), Grandfather Robert Jackson Martin and wife Mary (top right), Father Mickey Jackson Martin and wife Virginia, and Damen Jackson Martin

SINGER-COMPOSER
DAMEN JACKSON MARTIN

Articles about Damen's song "West of Tucumcari" have appeared in Route 66 Magazine, New Mexico Magazine, and Write-on Magazine. In addition, his song is one of those featured in an album published by the Tucumcari Chamber of Commerce entitled "Songs of Tucumcari." He has been hosted on two occasions by the Chamber for visits to the city. For information about either CD, contact Mike Martin of The Fowble Press.

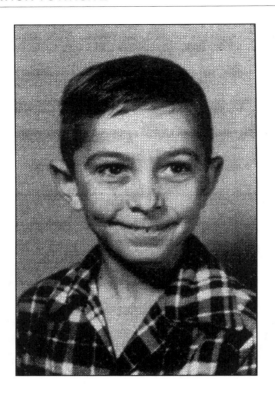

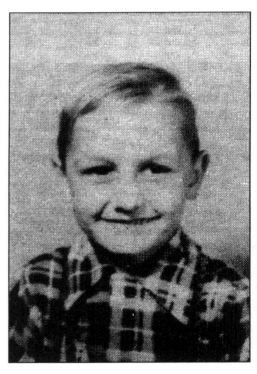

BROTHERS MICKEY (TOP), DICKEY (LEFT), AND BOBBY MARTIN
BRYANT ELEMENTARY SCHOOL – 1953

CHAPTER 12

BRYANT TOWN
AND SCHOOL REUNIONS

Bryant and Bryant School haven't been forgotten by everyone, not quite yet, anyway; memories of them live on in the hearts and minds of at least two different but overlapping groups of people. They live on, for example, in the minds of people like me—folks who either used to live at Bryant or attended or taught school there or had some other sort of personal or family or business tie to the area. Today, those who belong to this particular interest group live, for the most part, in other towns or counties or, in many cases, as far away as other states. Their interest in Bryant and Bryant School will last for the rest of their lives.

Interest in Bryant also lives on in the minds of yet another group of people—folks who, again, like me, have an abiding interest in the town site development period of the history of the State of Oklahoma. Members of this group are to be found in every state of the Union. Oklahoma, after all, is a state with an undeniably unique and interesting history, one that captured the minds of people in the old days and that continues to do so today.

What members of both groups have in common is an understanding of the fact that Bryant is representative of a large number of other communities that were just like it in their day—small farm towns that were brought into being at a time when land in the Oklahoma Indian Territory first became available for settlement by non-Indian outsiders. It is for this reason that whenever Bryant town or school reunions are held, people are apt to show up from almost anywhere in the country. Their presence, of course, is one of the reasons why Bryant reunions are not only interesting and educational but also a lot of fun!

BRYANT HIGH SCHOOL
REUNION OF JUNE 4, 1944

AN EARLY BRYANT SCHOOL REUNION
(EXACT DATE UNKNOWN)

Jack Reddick, Gary Muehlhansen (back), Dorothy Reddick, Durward Chancey (back to camera), George Reddick, Jackie Chancey, Juanita Middleton, George Brison, Ramona Cowan, and Dudley Hardin. Names may be out of order.

*Mary (West) Newman, Opal Chancey, Ted Chancey,
and Margie Coleman at the Bryant Reunion of 2000*

*Sibyl Chancey and Mike Martin
at a Bryant All-School Reunion*

TOP LEFT
Woodrow Wilkie
TOP CENTER
Unnamed
TOP RIGHT
Jimmie Smith
LEFT CENTER
Floyd Bowen
RIGHT CENTER
Charlie James
BOTTOM LEFT
Unnamed
BOTTOM CENTER
Bill Taber
BOTTOM RIGHT
Lonnie Kub

REUNION OF 2000

SCENE FROM THE REUNION OF 2000

DOROTHY JETTY (WEST) KIZER
Dorothy West is a former Bryant School student who earned a Master's from the University of Oklahoma and a Doctorate in Home Economics Education from Iowa State University and then went on to become an accomplished instructor and the author of several scholarly papers in her field of expertise.

TOP LEFT
Donald Chancey
TOP CENTER
Kenneth Popejoy
TOP RIGHT
Unnamed
LEFT CENTER
Winford Chancey
RIGHT CENTER
Glover Mainard
BOTTOM LEFT
Donald Chancey
BOTTOM CENTER
Richard Campbell
BOTTOM RIGHT
Unnamed

REUNION OF 2000

JOE J. STRUCKLE — CLASS OF 1952
(IN 1952 AND IN 2000)

CLASSROOM IN THE JOE J. STRUCKLE EDUCATION CENTER
AT NORTHWESTERN OKLAHOMA STATE UNIVERSITY IN ALVA, OK

JOE J. STRUCKLE EDUCATION CENTER

Dr. Joe J. Struckle, Bryant High School Class of 1952, retired as President of Northwestern Oklahoma State University at Alva in June of 2000. At that time, a building was renamed the Joe J. Struckle Education Center in honor of his service as president from 1975 to 2000.

The Struckle family at the building dedication ceremony and an interior view of the Joe J. Struckle Education Center

TOP LEFT
Unnamed
TOP CENTER
Wanda Horner
TOP RIGHT
Velva Bowen
LEFT CENTER
Juanita Middleton
RIGHT CENTER
Marguerite Horner
BOTTOM LEFT
Unnamed
BOTTOM CENTER
Gladys Wilkie
BOTTOM RIGHT
Donald James

REUNION OF 2000

*Martha Belle Davis
and her brothers
at Bryant*

*Martha Belle Davis
Bryant School
Class of 1944*

*Martha Belle (Davis) Schnabel,
as a young married woman*

Martha B. (Davis) Schnabel
Police Academy Graduate

Martha B. (Davis) Schnabel
Jail Crew, City of San Antonio, Texas
September, 1958

MARTHA BELLE (DAVIS) SCHNABEL

Martha was featured on the cover of Texas Police Officer Magazine as the first female police officer of the City of San Antonio, Texas. Note, too, that she has described her life experience in a book entitled "Officer Mama." Information about the book is available through Mike Martin of The Fowble Press.

Officer
Martha Belle (Davis) Schnabel
in uniform

County Judge
Martha Belle (Davis) Schnabel
Wilson County, Texas

TOP LEFT
Unnamed
TOP CENTER
Jackie (Houghton) Chancey
TOP RIGHT
Sibyl Chancey
LEFT CENTER
Unnamed
RIGHT CENTER
Florene Chancey
BOTTOM LEFT
Unnamed
BOTTOM CENTER
Ted Chancey and
Wanda McPherron
BOTTOM RIGHT
Unnamed

REUNION OF 2000

*George and Dorothy (West) Kaiser
at the Reunion of 2000*

*Elementary School Classmates
Pat Wasson, Jackie Satawake, and Mike Martin
at a Bryant All-School Reunion*

BRYANT HIGH SCHOOL

Exact year unknown

CHAPTER 13

BRYANT TODAY

In the absence of accounts like this one, there is little doubt that the stories of Bryant and Bryant School would fade away almost completely. Strangers who travel today through the area where they were located would almost certainly assume that the town and school have been long forgotten, since there's really nothing left of either one to be seen. The stores, schools, post office, telephone exchange, and all but a few of the old homes that used to make up the community have long since fallen into ruins and disappeared. The only landmarks still standing are a few of the older homes and the lovely little Bryant Community Church.

It was the blunt reality of a tax base not being adequate to meet the basic necessities of town life such as an adequate water system, social services, street maintenance, fire protection, law enforcement, schools, and so on that caused Bryant to fade away as it did. It's a shame, really, that more of the old town isn't still standing, since there are many parallels between what happened there and the raft of problems confronting communities all around our country today. Maybe they could learn something from what took place at towns like Bryant.

On a daily basis, stories appear in the media about towns and cities and counties that are struggling with the same fundamental problems that small farm towns such as Bryant had to deal with in the old days. Many small Oklahoma town sites like Bryant were devastated as our nation stumbled through the relatively rapid transformation from an agricultural to an industrial economy, and by studying their experiences, insights might be formed to help us deal with the transition taking place in our own time--the even more bewildering change from an industrial to an information society. Whether or not the civic entities of our times will be any more successful in terms of preventing failures than people were in the old days is very much an open question.

For the foreseeable future, the location of the Town of Bryant is likely to remain no more than an obscure marker that shows up on some maps of rural Okmulgee County. The average person would certainly have to be looking for the old town site to find it, that's for sure, since the area where it was located isn't visible from any heavily traveled road. And, once the site is physically located, it will become clear in only a minute that there isn't much left of the old town to be seen. Given its location a few miles southwest of the Town of Henryetta (which is itself located about 70 miles south of Tulsa near the intersection of the Indian

Nation Turnpike and Interstate Highway 40), only those who really want to see the location would have any reason to go there today.

Even so, for those who know the basics about Bryant and Bryant School, just driving through the area is more than enough to evoke some powerful images of all that existed there in times past. Not only were many lives touched by Bryant and its schools, mini-versions of most of the events and episodes that make up the history of the State of Oklahoma were acted out at this little town site. The story of Bryant and its struggles makes us think of common roots and values, and what happened there provides a reminder of the fact that all the many needs we have in common are far more important than any of our differences. Many of those who came before us lived through experiences just like the one that played out at Bryant, and that's what makes the story of the town so fascinating!

****

INDEX

Ω

Made in the USA
Middletown, DE
23 March 2018